BEGINNERS GUIDE TO HERBAL TEAS, INFUSIONS & REMEDIES

EXPLORE 85+ RECIPES TO EMPOWER YOU ON YOUR HEALTH JOURNEY USING EASILY ACCESSIBLE MEDICINAL PLANTS

DIVINE GREEN LIFE

CONTENTS

FREE BONUSES FOR OUR READERS!

Want more herbs at your fingertips?
Scan the QR code below or visit https://www.
divinegreenlife.com to receive:
ULTIMATE HERBAL MEDICINE QUICK REFERENCE GUIDE

Valued at $37

- 33 Powerful Medicinal Plants and their uses
- How to Create a Powerful Apothecary in your own Kitchen
- Take Your Health in Your Own Hands

ULTIMATE HERBAL MEDICINE QUICK REFERENCE PRINTABLE POSTER

Valued at $17

SCAN ME

JOIN OUR COMMUNITY OF LIKE-MINDED HERB-LOVING HUMANS!

Have questions? Want to share your creations with others? Connect with us in our private herbal community on Facebook by scanning the code below with your camera, see you on the inside!

Herbalism and Natural Living for Beginners

Private group · 1.7K members

"There are no incurable diseases
—only the lack of will.
There are no worthless herbs
—only the lack of knowledge."
~ Avicenna

HERBAL TEA RECIPES FOR BEGINNERS

Although they are available over the counter, aspirin, acetaminophen (paracetamol), and diphenhydramine—a familiar remedy for allergies, hay fever, or the common cold—result in some rather horrible side effects ranging from gastrointestinal bleeds, liver failure, and dizziness or drowsiness and impaired concentration. Not to mention that some of these medications lead to drug dependencies, addictions, and in extreme cases, abuse and overdose.

Unfortunately, aches and pains, allergies, illness, and inflammation are part of being human. In this modern age, we seem to be programmed to reach for conventional medication to beat the symptoms. But what if there were an alternative treatment that was perfectly natural? ...like herbs?

You don't need to be an herbalist or belong to some sort of woo-woo society to incorporate herbal alternatives into your daily healthcare and well-being routine. In fact, all you need to do is read this book and make yourself a cuppa tea (or three).

Celebrity doctor Andrew Weil, an advocate of alternative practices and herbal supplements, is tactful in his opinions of complementary medicine. He believes there should be a balance between conventional practices and alternative methods because, quite simply, some conditions can't be cured with vitamins and herbal syrups.

Weil explains his theory: "If I'm in a car accident, don't take me to an herbalist. If I have bacterial pneumonia, give me antibiotics. But when it comes to maximizing the body's natural healing potential, a mix of conventional and alternative procedures seems like the only answer" (Kluger, 1997).

In this book, we aim to show you, for example, how white willow bark can be used instead of aspirin; feverfew can be used instead of paracetamol; and goldenrod can be used to treat allergies, hay fever, and the symptoms of the common cold. Furthermore, we present how herbs like turmeric, ashwagandha, and ginger can not only assist with your current daily well-being, but also lead to continued good health. However, throughout, we encourage you to always seek professional medical advice before you start taking anything new, especially if you are already on medication or have an existing health condition.

Have you noticed that people seem to be getting more ill as stress levels increase and the quality of life takes a dive? Do you find the costs of conventional healthcare are getting out of hand? Are you concerned for the health of future you? How can we ensure that we age 'well' so that we can look forward to our senior years rather than dreading them and all the complications they can bring, like brain degeneration, arthritis, and other ailments? We believe the answers to those questions can be found in Mother Nature's pantry.

Finding health and wellness in all that nature provides is a wonderful thing. Herbs—and in this instance, *herbal teas*—have the capacity to offer relief from health conditions and promote greater health and wellness to assure us of a healthier future.

Nobody should struggle with their health and well-being when the Earth provides everything we need to live long, healthy lives. If conventional medicine has let you down, if traditional healthcare is becoming too costly, or if you simply want to embrace a more natural way, you will discover the well-researched information in this book—backed with references to scientific evidence—to be a practical and illuminating guide to greater health.

After years of researching alternatives to conventional medicine, with an emphasis on living healthfully and aging well, we have determined that nature has provided a bounty of health-care ingredients. As you explore alternative options like herbs and herbal teas, do so with the understanding that conventional is not all bad and natural doesn't always mean harmless. So, even though you don't need to be an herbalist, you do need to know some basics. Cue this book!

WHAT CAN YOU LOOK FORWARD TO?

In this book, you will find more than 80 herbal tea recipes, many of which are multi-ingredient teas that can be enjoyed as single-ingredient teas, boosting the total number of recipes well into the hundreds! And with every recipe, we list the potential health benefits of each herbal ingredient.

For your convenience, the recipes are organized into ten sections so that they are easy to differentiate and find. And, to make referencing even easier for you, at the end of each chapter, we provide a glossary with a brief summary of all the herbs mentioned.

The teas are divided into the following categories:

- Digestion and detoxification
- Immunity and stress relief
- Sleep and relaxation
- Women's health
- Skin and hair care
- Pain and inflammation relief
- Energy and focus
- Seasonal allergies
- Athletic performance
- Brain health

And be sure to look out for our bonus chapter, which is full of additional information, more tea recipes, and recipes for herbal tea smoothies!

Before we get to the recipes, we want to first share some information and insights that will make this book even more valuable to you, so don't just skip to the 'good stuff' without educating yourself first. Chapter 1 will introduce you to the benefits of herbs and drinking herbal teas; the different types of herbs, including energetics, classification, and the parts of the plant that are used; how to choose teas for your specific needs; safe blending practices; and the best way to prepare your tea for maximum benefit.

Shall we begin? Grab a cuppa, and let's get going!

BASIC PRINCIPLES OF HERBAL TEA

Herbal tea is a simple and natural way to enjoy the benefits of one of nature's finest gifts: herbs. Teas made with herbs have been used for centuries across various cultures to improve health and well-being. Herbal teas have a range of benefits, from calming the mind and reducing stress to aiding digestion and boosting immunity.

When it comes to selecting and preparing herbal teas, it is important to understand the different types of herbs and how to choose high-quality ingredients—all of which will be covered in this chapter.

By following a few simple steps, you can prepare a delicious and nourishing cup of herbal tea in just minutes... ah! How lovely.

Whether you are new to herbalism or an experienced herbalist, incorporating herbal teas into your daily routine can be an enjoyable and beneficial way to support your overall health and well-being.

AN OVERVIEW OF HERBAL TEA AND ITS BENEFITS

Herbal tea is an easy and convenient way to incorporate the health benefits of herbs into your diet and routine. It is also a great option for people who are concerned about their health, the growing cost of a well-balanced diet, and the impact and risks of conventional medicine.

With little to no side effects, herbal teas are an excellent way to improve your overall well-being. But, just to be safe, we will cover some cautionary information at the end of this chapter.

Studies have shown that herbs—in this case prepared as herbal teas—can help manage or sometimes even treat a variety of health issues. For example, chamomile tea can help with anxiety and insomnia (Srivastava et al., 2010), ginger tea can improve digestion and alleviate nausea (Ali et al., 2008), and peppermint tea can help with respiratory issues and headaches (McKay & Blumberg, 2006).

Herbal teas have been used for centuries in various cultures, including China, India, Japan, and Russia; we will read more about this presently.

We know now that the benefits of herbal teas are not limited to traditional medicine; findings from scientific studies support what tradition has long understood. For example, one study found that drinking green tea can help improve cardiovascular health (Babu, 2008), and another found that drinking chamomile tea can help reduce symptoms of anxiety.

Herbal teas can also be a cost-effective way to incorporate healthy habits into your daily routine. While fresh herbs can be expensive, dried herbs used for tea are often more affordable and can be found at most grocery stores. Of course, depending on where you live, you could also grow your own.

With a variety of herbs and flavors to choose from, there is a tea for everyone. So, why not take advantage of the health benefits of herbal teas and start incorporating them into your daily routine today?

Tea Tip

For the purposes of this book, the term herbal teas refers to all infusions from the bounty Mother Nature provides! This includes tea from the species Camellia sinensis (the species that gives us black and green tea), as well as all other herbs, spices, and even some fungi.

A BRIEF HISTORY OF HERBAL TEA AND ITS USES IN DIFFERENT CULTURES

Herbal tea has been used for centuries as a natural remedy and as a daily beverage in many cultures around the world. Each culture has its own unique herbal teas and rich traditions.

Let us explore the history and use of herbal tea in China, India, Japan, Russia, and the Western world.

The history of herbal tea in China

Traditional Chinese medicine has used herbs and herbal teas for over 5,000 years. Some of the most commonly used herbs in Chinese herbal teas include goji berry, chrysanthemum, and hawthorn berry. These herbs are believed to help boost the immune system, improve vision, and assist with heart health. In addition to their health benefits, herbal teas are also an important part of Chinese culture. They are served during social gatherings and gifted as a sign of respect to guests. ·

The history of herbal tea in India

In India, Ayurvedic medicine has used herbal teas for over 3,000 years to promote overall health. Ayurvedic teas are made with a variety of herbs, including turmeric, ginger, and holy basil. Amongst other things, these herbs are believed to help reduce inflammation, improve digestion, and boost the immune system. As with Chinese culture, herbal teas are also an important part of Indian culture.

The history of herbal tea in Japan

Japanese herbal teas, also known as *yu-cha*, are often made with herbs like green tea, licorice root, and ginger. These herbs are believed to help improve digestion, boost the immune system, and reduce inflammation. In Japan, herbal teas are an important part of traditional medicine and culture and are often served during tea ceremonies.

The history of herbal tea in Russia

Herbal teas have been used in Russia for centuries as a natural remedy and as a daily beverage. Russian herbal teas are also known as *zavarka*, and are often made with herbs like peppermint, chamomile, and rose hip. These herbs are believed to help improve digestion, reduce stress, and boost the immune system. In addition, herbal teas are an important part of Russian culture and are served during social gatherings.

The Western world and herbal tea

In the Western world, herbal tea has become increasingly popular in recent years as more people seek natural remedies and alternative solutions for their health concerns. Herbal teas are made with a variety of herbs that we'll explore as we make our way through this book. Generally, herbs are believed to help reduce stress, promote relaxation, and boost the immune system. In addition to their health benefits, herbal teas can be enjoyed as a daily beverage and are often used as a replacement for sugary drinks like soda.

Herbal tea has a rich history and is an important part of many cultures around the world. Whether you are looking to improve your health or simply enjoy a delicious and natural beverage, there is an herbal tea (or two) out there for you.

THE IMPORTANCE OF USING HIGH-QUALITY INGREDIENTS

When it comes to herbal teas, the quality of the ingredients used is crucial to achieving maximum health benefits. It's essential to use high-quality herbs that are free from pesticides, additives, and other harmful substances.

Research has shown that using high-quality ingredients in herbal teas can help improve overall health and wellness. For example, a study found that using high-quality herbs in traditional Chinese medicine resulted in better clinical outcomes compared to low-quality herbs (Marshall, 2020). A different study similarly found that using high-quality herbs in herbal teas led to better antioxidant and anti-inflammatory properties (Serafini, n.d.).

Most importantly, using high-quality herbs helps to ensure the safety of the tea and, therefore, the wellness of you, the tea drinker. Cheap or low-quality herbs can contain harmful contaminants, such as heavy metals and pesticides, which will be harmful to your health in the long term. It is essential to purchase herbs from a reputable source that guarantees the purity and quality of their products. And, since sourcing quality ingredients is crucial, consider growing your own; why not?

In addition to using high-quality herbs, it is important to store them properly to maintain their freshness and potency. Herbs should be stored in a cool, dark place away from moisture and light. Using airtight containers can also help to keep herbs fresh for longer.

Finally, when preparing your herbal tea, follow the recipe instructions carefully to achieve the best results and ensure that the tea is brewed correctly. Over-brewing or boiling herbs can destroy their beneficial properties and alter their taste.

Different herbs require different brewing times and temperatures; we will look at the 'how to' of making herbal teas a little later in this chapter, and each recipe will give you a guideline.

While on the subject of using high-quality ingredients, let's quickly probe the effects of adding sweeteners to herbal tea. Refined sugars negate the health benefits of herbs. Instead, try adding a natural sweetener, or enjoy your tea unsweetened. We will discuss the different types of sweetener alternatives in more detail in our bonus chapter, so stay tuned.

UNDERSTANDING THE DIFFERENT TYPES OF HERBS

There are many different types of herbs that can be used to make tea, each with its own unique set of properties and benefits. Understanding the different types of herbs and how they are classified can help you choose the best herbs for your intended purpose.

Different parts of plants can also be used to make herbal teas. Some teas use the leaves from the herb, such as peppermint and chamomile, while others use the roots, such as licorice and dandelion. Some herbs are harvested for their flowers, such as lavender and hibiscus, while others for their bark, such as cinnamon and willow. Understanding which parts of plants are used in herbal teas can help you choose the best herbs for your needs.

One important aspect of herbs is their energetics (Poswal, 2019). Energetics refer to the qualities and effects of herbs on the body and mind. Understanding the energetics of herbs can help you choose the best herbs to address specific health concerns. For example, cooling herbs such as peppermint and spearmint can be helpful for reducing inflammation and soothing digestive issues, while warming herbs such as ginger and cinnamon can be helpful for improving circulation and reducing pain.

Another important aspect of herbs is their classification. Herbs can be classified in many different ways: by their actions on the body, their taste, or their traditional use (Poswal, 2019). One common classification system for herbs is based on their medicinal properties. This system categorizes herbs into different groups based on their primary actions on the body, such as diuretic herbs that promote urine flow, nervine herbs that support the nervous system, or adaptogenic herbs that help the body adapt to stress.

To follow are some examples of different types of herbs that can be used to make herbal teas.

Cooling herbs

These herbs have a cooling and calming effect on the body. Examples include peppermint, spearmint, chamomile, and lemon balm.

Warming herbs

These herbs have a warming and invigorating effect on the body. Examples include ginger, cinnamon, cardamom, and turmeric.

Nervine herbs

These herbs have a calming and soothing effect on the nervous system. Examples include skullcap, passionflower, and valerian.

Adaptogenic herbs

These herbs help the body adapt to stress and promote overall wellness. Examples include ashwagandha, rhodiola, and holy basil.

Diuretic herbs

These herbs promote urine flow and can be helpful in supporting kidney function and reducing fluid retention. Examples include dandelion, parsley, and nettle.

When choosing herbs for your tea, it's important to consider your individual needs and health concerns. Also consider how herbs react with modern medicine or any prescriptions you may be taking and what the contraindications may be. But we will discuss this in-depth at the end of this chapter.

HOW TO CHOOSE THE RIGHT HERBS FOR DIFFERENT NEEDS

Choosing the right herbs for your needs is an important aspect of making herbal tea. Different herbs can have different benefits, and knowing which ones to use can make all the difference. Here are some tips on how to choose the right herbs for different needs:

First, identify your needs or goals. Are you looking to relax and reduce stress? Do you need help with digestion, or do you want to boost your immune system? Once you have identified your needs, you can then choose herbs that have properties that align with your goals.

Next, consider the taste and aroma of the herbs. Some herbs have a strong, bitter taste that may not be enjoyable for everyone. Other herbs have a more pleasant taste and aroma, making them easier to drink. It's important to choose herbs that you enjoy drinking to ensure that you will drink them regularly.

Lastly, consider any potential interactions with medications or existing health conditions. Always speak to a healthcare professional before starting to use herbal teas if you have any health concerns or take any medications.

Here is a quick guide to pairing herbs with different needs:

- For relaxation and stress relief, try chamomile, lavender, or passionflower. These herbs have calming properties and can help promote relaxation.
- For digestion, try ginger, peppermint, or fennel. These herbs can help soothe the digestive system and alleviate stomach discomfort.
- For immune support, try echinacea, elderberry, or ginger. These herbs can help boost the immune system and prevent illness.
- For energy and focus, try ginseng, yerba mate, or green tea. These herbs have stimulating properties and can help improve mental clarity and focus.
- For overall wellness, try nettle, dandelion, or burdock root. These herbs can help support the body's natural detoxification processes and promote overall health.

Remember, choosing the right herbs for your needs is just one aspect of making herbal tea. Also be sure to use high-quality ingredients and to follow proper brewing methods to ensure that you get the most benefits from your tea.

Pairing herbs to specific needs can be an easy and effective way to create your own personalized herbal tea blends.

HOW TO PREPARE HERBAL TEA

Generally, preparing herbal tea is a simple process that can be done in just a few steps. Here is a basic method for preparing herbal tea:

1. Boil water

Bring water to a boil in either a kettle or pot on the stovetop. Which of the two will depend on whether the herbs you're using need to be simmered or steeped.

2. Choose your herbs

Select the herbs you wish to use, either in the form of fresh or dry loose herbs or tea bags.

3. Measure herbs

Measure out the desired amount, typically one teaspoon of loose herbs or one tea bag per cup of water.

4. Steep or simmer the herbs

Some recipes require herbs to be simmered, while others should be steeped.

To simmer, place herbs into the water while it is boiling. Cover with a lid. Turn the heat down and allow the herbs to simmer for the time stated in the recipe.

To steep, once the water has come to a boil, remove the pot from the heat. Then, add the herbs and cover. Leave the herbs in the boiled water for as long as the recipe requires. Covering with a tea cozy at this point will prevent the tea from cooling too quickly, as some steeping times are as long as 15 minutes.

The simmering and steeping time depends on each herb's composition and flavor profile. For example, mild herbs like chamomile and hibiscus will require longer steeping times than peppermint. And 'harder' herbs like ginger and other roots will require longer steeping times than softer herbs.

5. Strain and enjoy

Remove the herbs and enjoy your freshly brewed tea! Finer ingredients like ground, dried cinnamon, and ginger may remain after straining, and that's okay; they can be ingested. Add lemon or a natural sweetener if you like. Don't use refined sugar. We will discover more about natural sweeteners in our bonus chapter.

By following these simple steps, you can create a delicious and nourishing cup of herbal tea in just minutes. Experiment with different herbs and blends to find the perfect combination for your needs and preferences.

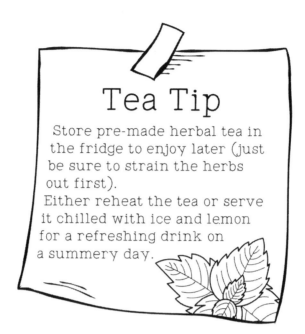

Tea Tip

Store pre-made herbal tea in the fridge to enjoy later (just be sure to strain the herbs out first).
Either reheat the tea or serve it chilled with ice and lemon for a refreshing drink on a summery day.

It is important to follow the specific instructions for the herbs you are using to ensure that you get the full benefit of the herbs and a delicious cup of tea. Additionally, some herbs may be more potent than others and require less heat to achieve the desired flavor and effect. By understanding the individual characteristics of each herb and following recommended brewing instructions, you can create the perfect cup of herbal tea. As we work through the recipes, this will become more evident.

Tea Tip

If you want stronger flavor profile, add more herbs rather than letting the tea brew for longer. Some herbs become bitter when steeped too long.

CAUTIONARY INFORMATION

While herbs have many health benefits when used properly, it is important to be cautious. Here are a few reasons why:

1. Interactions with medications

Herbs can interact with medications, either by enhancing or inhibiting their effects or by causing adverse reactions. It is important to talk to your healthcare provider before using herbs if you are taking medications.

2. Allergic reactions

Some people may be allergic to certain herbs and can experience symptoms such as itching, hives, or difficulty breathing. It is important to be aware of any allergies and to stop using an herb immediately if an allergic reaction occurs.

3. Overdose or toxicity

Some herbs can be toxic in large doses or if used improperly. For example, using too much of an herb like comfrey can cause liver damage, and using high doses of ephedra can cause heart problems. It is important to follow recommended dosage guidelines and to use herbs safely.

4. Quality and contamination

The quality and purity of herbs can vary widely, and some herbs may be contaminated with pesticides, heavy metals, or other harmful substances. As much as possible, try to purchase herbs from a reputable source and check for any certifications or testing. Growing your own herbs is also a great way to ensure they are fresh and of good quality!

It may be helpful to consult with a healthcare provider or a qualified herbalist before using herbs for any health concerns.

IS IT SAFE TO MAKE HERB BLENDS?

Blending herbs in herbal tea is generally safe, but it is important to consider the potential interactions between different herbs and any medications or medical conditions you may have. While herbal tea blends are generally considered safe, some herbs may have mildly toxic or harmful effects if used improperly or in large quantities. Be aware of potential adverse effects and use caution when combining multiple herbs in tea blends.

Furthermore, it is important to ensure that the herbs used in tea blends are high quality and free from contamination, as mentioned previously.

As with any herbal remedy, it is recommended to consult with a healthcare professional before using herbal tea blends, particularly if you are taking medications or have a medical condition.

What herbs should NOT be blended together in tea?

While many herbs blend nicely together in tea, there are some that should not be blended.

It is vitally important to consider any potential interactions between herbs and medications or medical conditions. For example, St. John's wort may interact with antidepressant medications, and licorice root may interact with medications for high blood pressure or heart disease. Consult with a healthcare provider before using herbs if you have any medical concerns or are taking medications.

Here is a quick comparative list of some of the herbs that must not be blended together:

- Stimulant herbs (yerba mate, ginseng) should not be blended with relaxing herbs (chamomile, valerian root).
- Diuretic herbs (dandelion, parsley) should not be blended with herbs that have moistening effects (marshmallow root, licorice root).
- Astringent herbs (witch hazel, yarrow) should not be blended with herbs that have nourishing effects (oat straw, nettle leaf).
- Herbs with estrogenic effects (red clover, dong quai) should not be blended with herbs that have anti-estrogenic effects (vitex, black cohosh).
- Blood-thinning herbs (ginger, turmeric) should not be blended with herbs that have blood-clotting effects (ginkgo, ginseng).

What herbs blend effectively together for herbal tea?

Different herbs blend nicely together for herbal tea depending on the desired flavor and effect. Some popular combinations include:

- Chamomile, lavender, and lemon balm for a calming, relaxing blend.
- Ginger, turmeric, and cinnamon for an immune-boosting, anti-inflammatory blend.
- Peppermint, lemon verbena, and licorice root for a soothing digestive blend.

- Elderberry, echinacea, and rose hips for an antioxidant-rich, immune-boosting blend.
- Rosemary, thyme, and sage for a refreshing, energizing blend.

Start with small amounts of each herb and adjust to taste, as some herbs may be more potent than others. Overall, experimenting with different herbal blends can be a fun and creative way to enjoy the benefits of herbal tea. Start with the many healthful, flavorful blends shared in the recipes in this book.

WRAPPING UP CHAPTER 1

Herbal teas are a delicious and beneficial way to incorporate herbs into your diet. They have been used for centuries across various cultures and can have a range of health benefits, including reducing stress, boosting immunity, aiding digestion, and more.

Choosing high-quality ingredients and understanding the different types of herbs can help you get the most out of your herbal teas. With some knowledge and a little experimentation, you can discover the perfect herbal teas and blends for your needs and preferences.

CHAPTER 1 GLOSSARY

Ashwagandha: Adaptogenic, helps the body adapt to stress, and promotes overall wellness.

Burdock root: Supports the body's natural detoxification processes and promotes overall health.

Cardamom: Warming and invigorating effect on the body.

Chamomile: Cooling and calming effect on the body, promotes relaxation, helps with digestion.

Cinnamon: Its bark is used in making herbal teas; warming and invigorating effect on the body, helps improve circulation and reduce pain.

Dandelion: Diuretic. Promotes urine flow and supports kidney function, reduces fluid retention, supports the body's natural detoxification processes, and promotes overall health.

Echinacea: Boosts the immune system and prevents illness.

Elderberry: Boosts the immune system and prevents illness.

Fennel: Helps soothe the digestive system and alleviate stomach discomfort.

Ginger: Warming and invigorating effect on the body, helps improve circulation and reduce pain, helps soothe the digestive system and alleviate stomach discomfort, boosts the immune system, and prevents illness.

Ginseng: Stimulates energy and focus and improves mental clarity.

Green tea: Stimulates energy and focus and improves mental clarity.

Hibiscus: Loaded with vitamin C. Has been found to have anxiolytic (anxiety-reducing) effects and can help lower blood pressure.

Holy basil: Adaptogenic, helps the body adapt to stress and promotes overall wellness.

Lavender: Promotes relaxation.

Lemon balm: Cooling and calming effect on the body.

Licorice: Digestive aid. Its anti-inflammatory properties can contribute to improved immune function.

Nettle: Diuretic. Promotes urine flow, supports kidney function, reduces fluid retention, supports the body's natural detoxification processes, and promotes overall health.

Parsley: Diuretic. Promotes urine flow, supports kidney function, and reduces fluid retention.

Passionflower: Calming and soothing effect on the nervous system, promotes relaxation.

Peppermint: Cooling effect on the body, reduces inflammation, and soothes digestive issues.

Rhodiola: Adaptogenic, helps the body adapt to stress and promotes overall wellness.

Skullcap: Calming and soothing effect on the nervous system.

Spearmint: Cooling effect on the body, reduces inflammation, soothes digestive issues.

Turmeric: Warming and invigorating effect on the body.

Valerian: Calming and soothing effect on the nervous system.

Willow: Contains salicin—similar to aspirin—and has anti-inflammatory and pain-relieving properties.

Yerba mate: Stimulates energy and focus and improves mental clarity.

Now, let's jump to the exciting part—the recipes!

HERBAL TEA FOR DIGESTION AND DETOX

The health of our digestive system is crucial to our overall well-being. When our gut is functioning optimally, we are able to effectively absorb the nutrients from our food and eliminate waste efficiently.

Factors such as poor diet, stress, and exposure to toxins can disrupt the delicate balance of our digestive system. Fortunately, there are many herbs that can aid in digestion and promote gut health.

In this chapter, we'll explore 10 delicious and easy-to-make herbal tea recipes that can help support digestive health and aid in the body's natural detoxification processes. From a refreshing lemon ginger detox tea to a soothing chamomile tea, these recipes offer a variety of flavors and health benefits to suit your taste buds and wellness goals. So, let's dip in and discover the power of herbal teas for digestive health and detox!

THE ROLE OF HERBS IN DIGESTIVE HEALTH

Herbs have been used for centuries to support digestive health, and they can play a valuable role in maintaining a healthy digestive system. Many herbs have digestive properties, including calming the stomach, easing bloating and gas, and promoting healthy bowel movements.

One herb that is commonly used for digestive health is ginger. Ginger has been shown to have anti-inflammatory properties, which can help soothe the stomach and reduce nausea. It can also help stimulate digestive enzymes and improve overall digestion. In one study, ginger was found to significantly reduce symptoms of indigestion and nausea in participants with functional dyspepsia (Richter, 2023).

Another herb that can be helpful for digestion is peppermint. Peppermint can help relax the muscles of the digestive tract, which can ease bloating and gas. It may also help relieve symptoms of irritable bowel syndrome (IBS), such as abdominal pain and discomfort. In one study, participants with IBS who took peppermint oil capsules for four weeks reported a significant reduction in symptoms compared to a placebo group (Alammar et al., 2019).

Fennel is another herb that can be beneficial for digestion. It has been shown to have anti-inflammatory and anti-spasmodic properties, which can help relieve gas, bloating, and abdominal pain. Fennel may also help stimulate the production of digestive enzymes and promote healthy bowel movements.

Tea Tip

Why do our recipes call for two cups of water?

Well, that's because tea is best shared with someone special.

Dandelion root can be helpful for digestion and detoxification. It has been traditionally used as a natural diuretic, which can help eliminate excess fluids from the body. Dandelion root also contains compounds that can help support liver function and promote healthy digestion.

Other herbs that can be helpful for digestive health include chamomile, licorice root, and turmeric. Chamomile has anti-inflammatory properties and can help soothe the stomach and promote healthy digestion. Licorice root has been shown to help reduce inflammation in the digestive tract and may also help relieve symptoms of acid reflux. Turmeric has been traditionally used to support healthy digestion and reduce inflammation.

It is important to remember that herbs are not a replacement for medical advice or treatment, and it is always a good idea to talk to your healthcare provider before using herbs for any health concerns.

Incorporating these herbs into your daily routine can be as simple as making a cup of herbal tea. You can use fresh or dried herbs or look for pre-made herbal tea blends that include these digestive herbs.

Now, let's take a look at some of those recipes, shall we?

RECIPES FOR HERBAL TEAS THAT AID DIGESTION AND PROMOTE DETOXIFICATION

1. Rooibos and Nettle Tea

Your ingredients:

- 1 bag rooibos tea
- 1-2 tsp dried nettle leaf
- 2 cups water

The best way to make it:

1. In a pot, bring water to a boil.
2. Add the rooibos and nettle leaves and let steep for 5-10 minutes.
3. Strain and serve.

A snippet of insight into the ingredients:

Originally from South Africa but now available worldwide, rooibos tea is packed with antioxidants and is believed to aid with digestion, amongst its other health benefits (Brown, 2023).

Nettle has anti-inflammatory properties and may help with allergies, joint pain, and digestive health. It is also a good source of vitamin C and minerals (Raman, 2022).

2. Lemon Ginger Detox Tea

Your ingredients:

- 1-inch fresh ginger root, sliced
- 1 lemon, sliced
- 2 cups water

The best way to make it:

1. In a pot, bring water to a boil.
2. Add ginger and lemon slices and simmer for 10 minutes.
3. Strain and serve.

A snippet of insight into the ingredients:

Ginger is a natural anti-inflammatory and can help reduce nausea, while lemon has detoxifying properties and can help with digestion and bloating.

3. Dandy Peppermint Tea

Your ingredients:

- 1 tsp dried peppermint leaf or 3-4 fresh peppermint leaves
- 1 tsp dried dandelion root
- 2 cups water

The best way to make it:

1. In a pot, bring water to a boil.
2. Add peppermint leaves and dandelion root and let steep for 5-10 minutes.
3. Strain and serve.

A snippet of insight into the ingredients:

Peppermint has been shown to relieve digestive issues such as bloating, gas, and stomach discomfort. Dandelion root can aid in liver detoxification and promote healthy digestion.

4. Three-in-One-Benefit Tea

Your ingredients:

- 1 tsp dried chamomile flower or 3-4 fresh chamomile flowers
- 1 tsp dried echinacea leaf or flower
- 2 cups water

The best way to make it:

1. In a pot, bring water to a boil.
2. Add chamomile flowers and echinacea and let steep for 5-10 minutes.
3. Strain and serve.

A snippet of insight into the ingredients:

The three-in-one properties of these ingredients include combined digestive aid. In addition, chamomile has calming properties, and echinacea is known for its immune-boosting properties that fight the symptoms of colds and flu.

5. Turmeric Ginger Tea

Your ingredients:

- 1-inch fresh ginger root, sliced
- 1 tsp ground turmeric
- 2 cups water

The best way to make it:

1. In a pot, bring water to a boil.
2. Add ginger and turmeric and allow to simmer for 10-15 minutes.
3. Strain and serve.

A snippet of insight into the ingredients:

Turmeric has anti-inflammatory properties and can help with liver detoxification, while ginger can help with digestion.

6. Digestive Harmony Tea

Your ingredients:

- 1 tsp fennel seed
- 1 tsp cumin seed
- 1 tsp coriander seed
- 2 cups water

The best way to make it:

1. In a pot, bring water to a boil.
2. Add the fennel, cumin, and coriander and simmer for 10 minutes.
3. Strain and serve.

A snippet of insight into the ingredients:

Fennel seed is used to treat digestive issues such as bloating, gas, and indigestion, while cumin seed has been shown to improve digestion and reduce inflammation. Coriander seed has also been used to treat digestive problems and has antioxidant properties.

7. Detox Tea

Your ingredients:

- 1 tsp dandelion root
- 1 tsp burdock root
- 1 tsp nettle leaf
- 2 cups water

The best way to make it:

1. In a pot, bring water to a boil.
2. Add dandelion root, burdock root, and nettle leaves.
3. Let the tea steep for 10-15 minutes.
4. Strain and serve.

A snippet of insight into the ingredients:

Dandelion root is a natural diuretic that can help to flush toxins from the body. Burdock root is also a natural detoxifier and can help to support liver function (an essential part of removing toxins from the body). Nettle leaves are rich in antioxidants, protecting the body from free radical damage and supporting overall detoxification.

QUICK TIPS FOR INCORPORATING HERBAL TEAS INTO A HEALTHY DIET

Herbal teas are a simple and delicious way to incorporate natural remedies into a healthy diet. They can be used to aid digestion, improve gut health, and promote overall well-being. Here are some tips for incorporating herbal teas into your daily routine:

1. **Choose teas with digestive benefits.** There are many herbs that can help with digestion, as we saw in the recipes above; ginger, fennel, and peppermint are the most frequently used. Choosing teas that contain these herbs can help alleviate digestive issues.
2. **Drink herbal tea before or after meals.** Drinking herbal tea before or after meals can help stimulate digestion and aid in the absorption of nutrients. For example, chamomile tea has been shown to improve digestion and reduce inflammation in the gut (Elliott, 2023). Drinking chamomile tea after a meal may also help reduce bloating and gas.
3. **Choose high-quality teas.** The quality and purity of herbs can vary widely, so it's important to purchase herbs and herbal teas from reputable sources. Look for teas that are certified organic and have undergone third-party testing for purity and quality.
4. **Experiment with different blends.** Herbal teas come in a variety of flavors and blends, so don't be afraid to experiment and find the ones that work best for you.

Refer to our guide in Chapter 1 for guidelines on how to blend herbs safely.

Tea Tip

Our tea blends are multi-functional, but several of the herbs in our blends can be used all on their own as a single-herb tea.

WRAPPING UP CHAPTER 2

You have 7 recipes in the bag that will aid digestive health and promote detoxification. In the next chapter, we'll investigate 7 more teas targeting immunity and stress relief.

CHAPTER 2 GLOSSARY

Burdock Root: Burdock root is a natural detoxifier that supports liver function and aids in removing toxins from the body.

Chamomile: Chamomile has anti-inflammatory properties, soothes the stomach, and promotes healthy digestion.

Coriander: Coriander treats digestive problems, has antioxidant properties, and supports overall digestive health.

Cumin: Cumin improves digestion and reduces inflammation.

Dandelion Root: Dandelion root is a natural diuretic. It aids in eliminating excess fluids from the body, supports liver function, and promotes healthy digestion.

Echinacea: Echinacea is known for its immune-boosting properties and can aid digestion when combined with other ingredients.

Fennel: Fennel has anti-inflammatory and anti-spasmodic properties, relieves gas, bloating, and abdominal pain, and stimulates the production of digestive enzymes.

Ginger: Ginger has anti-inflammatory properties, soothes the stomach, reduces nausea, stimulates digestive enzymes, and improves digestion.

Licorice Root: Licorice root reduces inflammation in the digestive tract and may alleviate symptoms of acid reflux.

Nettle: Nettle has anti-inflammatory properties, aids in allergies, joint pain, and digestive health, and is a good source of vitamin C and minerals.

Peppermint: Peppermint relaxes the muscles of the digestive tract, eases bloating and gas, and may alleviate symptoms of irritable bowel syndrome (IBS).

Rooibos: Rooibos tea is packed with antioxidants and is believed to aid digestion and provide various health benefits.

Turmeric: Turmeric supports healthy digestion, reduces inflammation, and aids in liver detoxification.

HERBAL TEA FOR IMMUNITY AND STRESS RELIEF

With a growing focus on natural remedies for immunity and stress relief, herbal teas have become increasingly popular. There's nothing quite like a warm cup of herbal tea to comfort and warm you—while delivering essential nutrients and medicinal benefits to your body.

In this chapter, we'll explore 10 herbal tea recipes specifically formulated for immunity and stress relief. Each recipe contains a combination of herbs that work together to boost the immune system, reduce stress, and promote well-being.

THE IMMUNE-BOOSTING PROPERTIES OF HERBS

Every herb has unique properties, and some are particularly effective at boosting the immune system.

One of the most popular immune-boosting herbs is echinacea. Echinacea contains polysaccharides, which stimulate the immune system by activating white blood cells. A study published in The Lancet Infectious Diseases found that echinacea reduced the incidence of the common cold by 58% and reduced the duration of colds by 1.4 days on average (Shah et al., 2007).

Another powerful herb for immune support is elderberry. Elderberry is rich in flavonoids and anthocyanins, which have antioxidant and anti-inflammatory effects. A study published in the Journal of International Medical Research found that elderberry extract reduced the severity and duration of influenza symptoms (Tiralongo et al., 2016).

Ginger is also a potent immune-boosting herb. Ginger contains compounds called gingerols and shogaols, which have anti-inflammatory and antioxidant properties. A study published in the Journal of Ethnopharmacology found that ginger extract enhanced the immune system by increasing the production of T-cells and cytokines (Mashhadi et al., 2013).

These are just a few examples of the many immune-boosting herbs available. Incorporating herbs like echinacea, elderberry, and ginger into your diet, particularly in the form of herbal teas, can help support your immune system and promote overall health and wellness.

Whether you're looking to unwind after a long day, boost your immune system during cold and flu season, or enjoy the delicious flavors, these recipes have something for everyone. So, sit back, relax, and enjoy a cuppa while you read about the benefits of these nourishing and healing herbal teas.

RECIPES FOR HERBAL TEAS THAT SUPPORT IMMUNITY AND REDUCE STRESS

8. Flower-Filled Calming Tea

Your ingredients:

- 1/2 tsp dried chamomile flower or 3–4 fresh chamomile flowers
- 1/2 tsp dried passionflower leaf and flower
- 1/2 tsp dried rose hip
- 1/2 tsp dried hibiscus flower
- 2 cups water

The best way to make it:

1. In a pot, bring water to a boil.
2. Add the flowers and allow to steep for 5–10 minutes.
3. Strain and serve.

A snippet of insight into the ingredients:

Chamomile has anti-inflammatory properties that help reduce inflammation in the body. It also has a calming effect and helps reduce stress and anxiety.

Passionflower has been found to have anxiolytic effects and can help improve sleep quality. It has also been shown to have anti-depressant properties (Janda et al., 2020)

Rose hips are a good source of vitamin C, which can help boost the immune system and reduce stress (Davidson, 2019.)

Hibiscus has been found to have anxiolytic effects and can help lower blood pressure (Jalalyazdi et al., 2019).

9. Stress-Less Tea

Your ingredients:

- 1 tsp dried lemon balm leaf or 3–4 fresh lemon balm leaves
- 1 tsp dried ginseng root
- 2 cups water

Tea Tip

Substitute the ginseng with licorice root and you'll have a tea that has antiviral properties that help boost the immune system.

The best way to make it:

1. In a pot, bring water to a boil.
2. Add lemon balm leaf and ginseng root and let steep for 5–10 minutes.
3. Strain and serve.

A snippet of insight into the ingredients:

Lemon balm and ginseng have a calming effect and help reduce stress and anxiety. In addition, lemon balm has antiviral properties and ginseng has anti-inflammatory and antioxidant properties that help boost the immune system.

10. Anti-Inflamma-Tea

Your ingredients:

- 1-inch fresh ginger root, sliced
- 1 tsp ground turmeric
- 1 tsp chamomile
- 2 cups water

The best way to make it:

1. In a pot, bring water to a boil.
2. Add ginger, turmeric, and chamomile and let simmer for 10–15 minutes.
3. Strain and serve.

A snippet of insight into the ingredients:

Turmeric has anti-inflammatory properties that help reduce inflammation in the body. It also has antioxidant properties that help boost the immune system. Ginger has anti-inflammatory properties that help reduce stress and anxiety. Chamomile helps reduce inflammation in the body.

11. Happy Mood Tea

Your ingredients:

- 1 tsp dried lavender flower
- 1 tsp dried lemon balm leaf
- 2 cups water

The best way to make it:

1. In a pot, bring water to a boil.
2. Add dried lavender flowers and lemon balm leaves and let steep for 5–10 minutes.
3. Strain and serve.

A snippet of insight into the ingredients:

Lavender has been shown to have calming and soothing effects on the body and mind, while lemon balm has been found to have anxiolytic and mood-enhancing properties (Koulivand, 2013).

12. Immune Booster Tea

Your ingredients:

- 1 tsp dried echinacea root
- 1 tsp dried elderberry
- 1 tsp dried rose hip
- 2 cups water

Tea Tip

Any of our multi-herb tea ingredients can be made into a single-herb tea.

Simply keep the herb-to-water ratio the same.

The best way to make it:

1. In a pot, bring water to a boil.
2. Add echinacea root, elderberries, and rose hips, and simmer for 10–15 minutes.
3. Strain and serve.

A snippet of insight into the ingredients:

Echinacea is known to support the immune system by stimulating white blood cells to fight off infection. Elderberries are high in antioxidants and have antiviral properties that help reduce symptoms of cold and flu (Sipsby, n.d.). Rose hips are rich in vitamin C, which helps boost the immune system.

13. Low Stress High Immuni-Tea

Your ingredients:

- 1 tsp dried ashwagandha root
- 1 tsp dried ginger root
- 1 tsp dried licorice root
- 2 cups water

Tea Tip

Ashwagandha tea bags are available from grocery or health food stores.

The best way to make it:

1. In a pot, bring water to a boil.
2. Add the ashwagandha, ginger, and licorice root.
3. Reduce heat and let the mixture simmer for 10–15 minutes.
4. Strain and serve.

A snippet of insight into the ingredients:

Ashwagandha is a traditional Ayurvedic herb that has been used for centuries for its stress-reducing and immune-boosting properties. Studies have shown that ashwagandha can help reduce anxiety and cortisol levels, which can contribute to improved immune function (Kubala, 2022).

Ginger and licorice root are also known for their anti-inflammatory properties and can help support immune function (Wahab et al., 2021).

14. Holy Harmony Tea

Your ingredients:

- 1 tsp dried holy basil leaf
- 1 tsp dried chamomile flower
- 1 tsp dried lemon balm leaf
- 2 cups water

The best way to make it:

1. In a pot, bring water to a boil.
2. Add the holy basil leaves, chamomile flowers, and lemon balm leaves.
3. Reduce heat and let the mixture simmer for 5–10 minutes.
4. Strain and serve.

A snippet of insight into the ingredients:

Holy basil, also known as tulsi, has been used in Ayurvedic medicine for its immune-boosting and stress-reducing properties. Studies have shown that holy basil can help reduce stress and anxiety and may also have antibacterial and antiviral properties (Cohen, 2014). Chamomile and lemon balm are also known for their calming properties and can help reduce stress and anxiety (Health Library, n.d.)

TIPS FOR MANAGING STRESS AND ANXIETY WITH HERBAL TEAS

In today's fast-paced world, it's easy to become overwhelmed and stressed. The constant demands of work, relationships, and other aspects of life can take a toll on both our physical and mental health. Fortunately, nature has provided us with a bounty of herbs that can help us manage stress and anxiety. One simple and enjoyable way to incorporate these herbs into our daily routine is with herbal teas.

By taking the time to sit down and enjoy a warm cup of herbal tea, we can help reduce our stress levels and promote a sense of calm and relaxation. So next time you're feeling overwhelmed, consider reaching for a cup of tea to help soothe your mind and body.

WRAPPING UP CHAPTER 3

Now you have 14 recipes under your belt! The first 7 are to aid with digestive health and promote detoxification, and then we had 7 specifically targeted at immunity and stress relief. In the next chapter, we'll discover another 7 teas. These are aimed at sleep and relaxation.

CHAPTER 3 GLOSSARY

Ashwagandha: Stress-reducing, immune-boosting, reduces anxiety and cortisol levels.

Chamomile: Anti-inflammatory, calming, and reduces stress and anxiety.

Echinacea: Stimulates the immune system and reduces the incidence and duration of the common cold.

Elderberry: Rich in antioxidants, reduces the severity and duration of influenza symptoms.

Ginger: Contains compounds with anti-inflammatory and antioxidant properties, enhances the immune system.

Ginseng: Calming, reduces stress and anxiety, and has anti-inflammatory and antioxidant properties.

Hibiscus: Anxiolytic, helps lower blood pressure.

Holy Basil (Tulsi): Immune-boosting, stress-reducing, antibacterial, and antiviral properties.

Lavender: Calming and soothing effects on the body and mind.

Lemon Balm: Calming, reduces stress and anxiety, antiviral properties.

Licorice Root: Anti-inflammatory, supports immune function.

Passionflower: Anxiolytic, improves sleep quality, and may have antidepressant properties.

Rose hip: Good source of vitamin C, boosts the immune system, and reduces stress.

Turmeric: Anti-inflammatory, antioxidant, boosts the immune system.

4

HERBAL TEA FOR SLEEP AND RELAXATION

If you need help winding down after a busy day or have trouble sleeping, herbal teas may be the solution. In this chapter, we'll share another 7 recipes for herbal teas. This time, targeted at helping you achieve a peaceful and rejuvenating night's sleep. So, grab your favorite cup, get comfy, and let's get started!

THE BENEFITS OF HERBAL TEAS FOR SLEEP AND RELAXATION

A good night's sleep is vital for our mental and physical well-being. Not getting enough good, quality sleep can lead to a range of health problems, including fatigue, poor concentration, mood swings, and a weakened immune system. According to the National Sleep Foundation, adults should aim for seven to nine hours of sleep per night to function at their best (National Sleep Foundation, 2021).

If you're having trouble falling asleep or staying asleep, herbal teas may offer a natural solution. Unlike medications that can have unwanted side effects, herbal teas are safe and gentle on the body when used as directed. But don't be lulled into negligence, their effects are real, so please don't use them ad-lib.

Herbal teas have been used for centuries for their calming and relaxing properties, making them the perfect addition to any bedtime routine. For example, chamomile tea contains an antioxidant called apigenin, which has been shown to have a sedative effect on the body. Valerian root is another popular choice for its calming properties and ability to help improve sleep quality. It contains compounds that can help increase levels of GABA, a neurotransmitter that helps regulate sleep.

Another benefit of herbal teas is what we outlined in the previous chapter: they can help reduce stress and anxiety, which can be a significant factor in sleep disturbances. Herbs such as lavender and passionflower have been shown to have anxiolytic effects, helping to calm the mind and promote relaxation.

Overall, herbal teas can be an excellent natural solution for those struggling to relax or get a good night's sleep. With a range of herbs and blends available, there's sure to be a tea that helps you unwind and feel sleepy.

Tea Tip

Use the following herbal teas in moderation, with care, and in the comfort of your home, as they can cause drowsiness and impede concentration.

RECIPES FOR HERBAL TEAS THAT PROMOTE RESTFUL SLEEP AND RELAXATION

15. Valerian Root Tea

Your ingredients:

- 1–2 tsp dried valerian root
- 2 cups water

The best way to make it:

1. In a pot, bring water to a boil.
2. Add the dried valerian root to the pot.
3. Let steep for 5–10 minutes.

4. Strain and serve.

A snippet of insight into the ingredients:

Valerian root has been traditionally used as a natural sedative and sleep aid. It is believed to increase levels of GABA in the brain and help promote relaxation. Some people may find the taste of valerian root tea to be quite strong, so you may want to consider adding a natural sweetener like honey or stevia.

Tea Tip

Some herbs, like valerian, are potent and strong enough to be used as a standalone for their unique benefits.

16. Low-caffeine Green Tea

Your ingredients:

- 1–2 bags of low-caffeine green tea

The best way to make it:

1. In a pot, bring water to a boil.
2. Add the tea bags to the pot.
3. Let steep for 5 minutes.
4. Remove tea bags and serve.

A snippet of insight into the ingredients:

Green tea is believed to help support brain function and fat loss, help reduce the risk of heart disease, and offer some protection against cancer. In addition, research suggests that epigallocatechin–3-O-gallate (EGCG), which is found in green tea, could be the reason behind green tea's sedative effect (Singh, 2011). You will benefit from drinking green tea at any time of the day but be sure to choose a low-caffeine green tea if you are planning to drink it close to bedtime.

17. Hops Tea

Your ingredients:

- 1–2 tsp dried hops flowers
- 2 cups water

Tea Tip

Adding cinnamon, ground ginger, and/or ground nutmeg to any single-herb tea will provide additional health benefits.

The best way to make it:

1. In a pot, bring water to a boil.
2. Add the dried hops flowers to the pot.
3. Let steep for 5–10 minutes.
4. Strain and serve.

A snippet of insight into the ingredients:

Hops is a bitter herb used in the brewing of beer, but it is also an effective sleep aid. The flowers of the hops plant contain a compound called humulene, which has sedative properties. Because it is naturally bitter, you may want to add a natural sweetener like honey or stevia.

18. Calm and Sleepy Tea

Your ingredients:

- 1 tsp dried skullcap
- 1 tsp dried passionflower leaf or flower
- 1 tsp dried lemon verbena leaf
- 2 cups water

The best way to make it:

1. In a pot, bring water to a boil.
2. Add the dried lemon verbena, skullcap, and passionflower to the pot.
3. Let steep for 5–10 minutes.
4. Strain and serve.

A snippet of insight into the ingredients:

Lemon verbena has a calming effect and can help with anxiety and stress.

Skullcap has a sedative effect and can help with anxiety and insomnia.

Passionflower is often used as a natural remedy for anxiety and sleep problems. It is believed to help increase levels of the neurotransmitter GABA, which promotes relaxation.

19. Lemon Balm and Magnolia Tea

Your ingredients:

- 1 tsp fresh or dried lemon balm leaves
- 1 tsp dried magnolia
- 2 cups water

The best way to make it:

1. In a pot, bring water to a boil.
2. Add the lemon balm leaves and magnolia to the pot.
3. Let steep for 5–10 minutes.
4. Strain and serve.

A snippet of insight into the ingredients:

Lemon balm is a member of the peppermint family and is known for its calming properties. It has been traditionally used to help reduce anxiety and promote relaxation.

Made from the dried buds, stems, and bark of the magnolia plant, magnolia tea is used as a sleep aid in many forms of traditional medicine.

20. Lavender Chamomile Tea

Your ingredients:

- 1 tsp dried lavender
- 1–2 tsp dried chamomile flower
- 2 cups water

The best way to make it:

1. In a pot, bring water to a boil.
2. Add the dried lavender and chamomile flowers to the pot.
3. Let steep for 5–10 minutes.
4. Strain and serve.

A snippet of insight into the ingredients:

Lavender has been shown to improve sleep quality and reduce anxiety, while chamomile has a calming effect and can help with insomnia.

21. Moon Milk

Your ingredients:

- 1/2 tsp ground ashwagandha powder
- 1 tsp coconut oil
- 1/2 tsp ground cinnamon or a cinnamon stick
- 1/4 tsp ground ginger

- a pinch of ground nutmeg
- 1 cup milk of your choice (whole, almond, coconut, etc.)

The best way to make it:

1. Bring the milk to a simmer.
2. Once the milk is hot, add the ashwagandha, cinnamon, ginger, and nutmeg, and whisk it together.
3. Gently simmer for 5 minutes.
4. Stir in the coconut oil and pour the moon milk into a cup.

Tea Tip

On its own, ashwa-gandha makes a great herbal tea. Simply brew 1 tsp ashwagandha powder in 2 cups of boiled water and allow it to steep for 5-10 minutes. Strain and serve.

A snippet of insight into the ingredients:

Studies have found that ashwagandha has the potential to help the body unwind, relax, prepare for rest, and improve overall sleep quality (Langade et al., 2019).

Cinnamon, ground ginger, and ground nutmeg have been used for centuries to aid relaxation and improve sleep quality. Cinnamon contains cinnamaldehyde, which has been found to have sedative effects and may help regulate sleep cycles. Ground ginger promotes better digestion, which can reduce discomfort and improve sleep quality. And ground nutmeg contributes to relaxation and better sleep thanks to a compound called myristicin.

TIPS FOR IMPROVING SLEEP HYGIENE AND CREATING A RELAXING BEDTIME ROUTINE

According to the Sleep Foundation, paying attention to sleep hygiene is one of the simplest ways to ensure better sleep (Suni, 2023).

Good sleep hygiene means having daily routines and a bedroom environment that promote uninterrupted sleep. Building healthy habits during the day, keeping to a consistent sleep schedule, ensuring your room is comfortable and free of disruptions, and following a pre-bedtime routine all contribute to ideal sleep hygiene.

Poor sleep hygiene and inadequate sleep can lead to a range of health issues, including obesity, cardiovascular disease, and depression. In this section, we'll cover some tips for improving your sleep hygiene:

1. **Stick to a consistent sleep schedule.** Help regulate your body's sleep-wake cycle by going to bed and waking up at the same time each day, even on weekends.
2. **Create a calming bedtime routine.** Read, take a warm bath, listen to soothing music, or practice other relaxing activities before bed. This will let your body know it's time to wind down.
3. **Create a sleep-conducive environment.** Use comfortable bedding, invest in a good quality mattress and pillows, and make sure your bedroom is cool, quiet, and dark.
4. **Limit caffeine and alcohol intake.** Caffeine and alcohol can disrupt sleep, so it's best to avoid them before bedtime.
5. **Avoid using electronic devices before bed.** The blue light emitted by electronic devices can suppress melatonin production and interfere with sleep.
6. **Consider drinking herbal teas.** As detailed in the recipes above, some herbal teas have been found to promote relaxation and improve sleep quality.
7. **Incorporate relaxation techniques.** Prayer, meditation, deep breathing, and progressive muscle relaxation are all practices that can soothe and calm the body and mind.

Improve your sleep hygiene and increase your chances of getting a restful night's sleep by incorporating these seven tips into your daily routine.

WRAPPING UP CHAPTER 4

Well, that brings us to a total of 21 recipes! We are well on our way to having an herbal tea for every occasion: aiding with digestive health and detoxification, immunity and stress relief, and sleep and relaxation. In the next chapter, we'll discover another 7 teas. These are aimed at women's health.

CHAPTER 4 GLOSSARY

Ashwagandha: Helps the body unwind, relax, and prepare for rest, improving sleep quality.

Chamomile: Calming herb, helps with insomnia and promotes relaxation.

Cinnamon: Contains cinnamaldehyde, which has sedative effects and may help regulate sleep cycles.

Ginger: Promotes better digestion, reduces discomfort, and improves sleep quality.

Green Tea: Contains compounds, such as EGCG, that may have a sedative effect and promote relaxation. Choose low-caffeine green tea for bedtime consumption.

Hops: Contains humulene, a compound with sedative properties, which aids in sleep.

Lavender: Improves sleep quality and reduces anxiety.

Lemon Balm: Calming herb, reduces anxiety and promotes relaxation.

Lemon Verbena: Calming herb, helps with anxiety and stress.

Magnolia: Used as a sleep aid, promotes relaxation.

Nutmeg: Contributes to relaxation and better sleep.

Passionflower: Natural remedy for anxiety and sleep problems, promotes relaxation.

Skullcap: Sedative herb that helps with anxiety and insomnia.

Valerian Root: Natural sedative and sleep aid, promotes relaxation.

HERBAL TEA FOR WOMEN'S HEALTH

For centuries, herbal teas have been used in various cultures as a natural approach to supporting women's health. In this chapter, we will explore the role of herbs in promoting women's health and the benefits they offer in addressing specific concerns, including hormonal balance, menstrual health, perimenopause, and menopause. We'll discuss which herbs are best for women's well-being and discover some herbal teas that you can enjoy, easing you through some of these trying times.

THE ROLE OF HERBS IN WOMEN'S HEALTH

A woman's health is an incredibly complex part of her overall well-being. Throughout the different stages of life, she will experience physiological changes— through puberty, pregnancy, perimenopause, or menopause—that influence hormonal balance and, through that, myriad other aspects of her health. These changes can be difficult and disruptive; thankfully, Mother Nature provides all we need in the form of herbal remedies. Let's explore.

Herbs for hormonal balance and menstrual health

Chasteberry is a popular herb believed to help regulate menstrual cycles and alleviate symptoms of premenstrual syndrome (PMS) (Petre, 2023). Additionally, herbs such as dong quai and black cohosh have been used to support hormonal balance and provide relief from menstrual discomfort (Heitz, 2019).

Herbs for perimenopause and menopause

Perimenopause can bring about various physical and emotional changes, and it is believed that herbal teas can offer support. Maca has shown promise in reducing symptoms related to hormonal imbalance during perimenopause (Meissner et al., 2006), and red clover is commonly used to help alleviate menopausal symptoms such as hot flashes and night sweats (Kanadys et al., 2021).

Emotional well-being

Women's emotional well-being can be influenced by hormonal fluctuations. Fortunately, certain herbs are known for their calming and mood-enhancing properties. For example, St. John's wort has been used to alleviate symptoms of mild to moderate depression and promote a positive mood which may help reduce anxiety and promote relaxation (Pietrangelo, 2018).

Now, let's take a look at how we can incorporate these herbs and more into some herbal tea recipes.

RECIPES FOR HERBAL TEAS THAT SUPPORT HORMONAL BALANCE, MENSTRUAL HEALTH, PERIMENOPAUSE, AND MENOPAUSE

22. Hormonal Balance Tea

Your ingredients:

- 1 tsp chasteberry
- 1 tsp dong quai root
- 1 tsp red clover
- 2 cups water

The best way to make it:

1. In a pot, bring water to a boil.
2. Add the chasteberry, dong quai root, and red clover.
3. Let the herbs steep for 10–15 minutes.
4. Strain and serve.

A snippet of insight into the ingredients:

Chasteberry is believed to support hormonal balance in women. It acts on the pituitary gland, helping to regulate the production of hormones.

Dong quai root is also known as "female ginseng" and has been used in traditional Chinese medicine to support women's health.

Red clover contains phytoestrogens, which are plant compounds similar to estrogen. It is commonly used to support women's health during menopause.

23. Menstrual Health Tea

Your ingredients:

- 1 tsp raspberry leaf
- 1 tsp nettle leaf
- 1 tsp chamomile
- 2 cups water

The best way to make it:

1. In a pot, bring water to a boil.
2. Add the raspberry leaf, nettle leaf, and chamomile.
3. Allow the herbs to steep for 5–10 minutes.
4. Strain and serve.

A snippet of insight into the ingredients:

Raspberry leaf is believed to have toning and strengthening effects on the uterus.

Nettle leaf is a nutrient-rich herb that offers numerous benefits for women's health. It is used to support healthy menstrual cycles by helping to reduce menstrual pain and alleviate symptoms of PMS.

As we've noted before, chamomile is a soothing herb that offers stress relief and relaxation. It is often used to promote restful sleep and alleviate anxiety or nervousness.

24. Perimenopause Support Tea

Your ingredients:

- 1 tsp black cohosh root
- 1 tsp motherwort
- 1 tsp sage leaf
- 2 cups water

The best way to make it:

1. In a pot, bring water to a boil.
2. Add the black cohosh root, motherwort, and sage leaf.
3. Let the herbs steep for 10–15 minutes.
4. Strain and serve.

A snippet of insight into the ingredients:

Black cohosh root and sage leaf are both known for their potential to reduce the hot flashes, night sweats, and mood swings that are commonly experienced during perimenopause.

Motherwort is believed to offer calming and relaxing properties, which can help reduce anxiety and promote a sense of well-being.

25. Menopause Relief Tea

Your ingredients:

- 1 tsp dong quai root
- 1 tsp red clover
- 1 tsp licorice root
- 2 cups water

The best way to make it:

1. In a pot, bring water to a boil.
2. Add the dong quai root, red clover, and licorice root.
3. Allow the herbs to steep for 10–15 minutes.
4. Strain and serve.

A snippet of insight into the ingredients:

We have previously discussed the benefits of dong quai root and red clover for female hormonal health.

In the context of menopause, licorice root is known for its potential to support hormonal balance. It contains compounds called phytoestrogens that mimic the effects of estrogen in the body.

26. Hormone-Balancing Blend

Your ingredients:

- 1 tsp maca root powder
- 1 tsp shatavari root powder
- 1 tsp ashwagandha root powder
- 2 cups water

The best way to make it:

1. In a pot, bring water to a boil.
2. Add the maca root powder, shatavari root powder, and ashwagandha root powder.
3. Let the blend steep for 10–15 minutes.
4. Strain and serve.

A snippet of insight into the ingredients:

Maca root powder has gained popularity for its potential to support hormonal balance in women. It contains various compounds that may help regulate hormone production and balance estrogen and progesterone levels.

Shatavari, known as "the queen of herbs" in Ayurveda, is a popular herb for women's health. It is especially renowned for its ability to support hormonal balance and reproductive health.

While ashwagandha is primarily known for its stress-reducing properties. This action of lowering cortisol levels plays a role in balancing female hormones by lowering the body's stress response.

27. Uterine Tonic Tea

Your ingredients:

- 1 tsp red raspberry leaf
- 1 tsp nettle leaf
- 1 tsp rose petals
- 2 cups water

The best way to make it:

1. In a pot, bring water to a boil.
2. Add the red raspberry leaf, nettle leaf, and rose petals.
3. Allow the herbs to steep for 5–10 minutes.
4. Strain and serve.

A snippet of insight into the ingredients:

We have previously discussed the benefits of raspberry and nettle leaf for uterine health.

Rose petals, in this context, can also help tone and support the health of the uterus. They have been used traditionally to support hormonal balance in women and they are renowned for their soothing and calming properties.

28. Calming Menstrual Tea

Your ingredients:

- 1 tsp chamomile
- 1 tsp lemon balm
- 1 tsp lavender
- 2 cups water

Tea Tip

You can add chamomile, lemon balm, and lavender to any of the teas in this chapter for their additional calming properties.

The best way to make it:

1. In a pot, bring water to a boil.
2. Add the chamomile, lemon balm, and lavender.
3. Let the herbs steep for 5–10 minutes.
4. Strain and serve.

A snippet of insight into the ingredients:

We previously discussed the calming benefits of our ingredients. However, it's good to be reminded that at various stages in our lives, we may experience heightened stress and mood fluctuations—hormonal balance, our monthly cycle, perimenopause, and menopause being the focus of this section. At least we know that chamomile, lemon balm, and lavender can help alleviate these symptoms by aiding better sleep and promoting a sense of calm and tranquility.

TIPS FOR MANAGING WOMEN'S HEALTH ISSUES WITH HERBAL TEAS

As women, we must prioritize the utmost care and attention for our health and well-being. From supporting hormonal balance to easing menstrual discomfort, herbal teas can be a comforting and gentle companion on our journey.

Here are some tips for incorporating herbal teas into your routine to help you nurture and manage your feminine health:

1. **Find balance with hormone-supportive teas that contain herbs like chasteberry and dong quai root.**
2. **Embrace the power of adaptogens;** they are your invaluable allies in managing stress and promoting resilience. Herbal teas that contain maca root powder, shatavari root powder, and ashwagandha root powder can help balance hormones and support female reproductive health.
3. **Soothe menopausal symptoms with teas that contain black cohosh root, motherwort, and sage leaf.**
4. **Opt for teas that are formulated to support uterine health and menstrual well-being.** These will combine herbs such as red raspberry leaf, nettle leaf, and rose petals.
5. **Allow herbs to be your calming allies.** At any stage of our lives when we feel stressed and anxious, herbal teas can provide comfort. Prepare teas containing herbs like chamomile, lemon balm, and lavender.

Harnessing the power of nature, herbal teas can be a nurturing and empowering way to support women's health.

WRAPPING UP CHAPTER 5

Isn't it wonderful to know that there is an herbal tea for every occasion and condition? With 28 recipes to experiment with, you are well on your way to being an herbal tea aficionado! In the next chapter, we'll discover another 7 teas aimed at optimal skin and hair health.

CHAPTER 5 GLOSSARY

Ashwagandha: Helps regulate cortisol levels, indirectly impacting hormone balance.

Black Cohosh: Reduces hot flashes, night sweats, and mood swings during perimenopause.

Chamomile: Soothing herb that promotes restful sleep and alleviates anxiety or nervousness.

Chasteberry: Helps regulate menstrual cycles and alleviate symptoms of PMS.

Dong Quai: Supports hormonal balance and provides relief from menstrual discomfort.

Lavender: Improves sleep quality, reduces anxiety, and promotes relaxation.

Lemon Balm: Calming herb that reduces stress and promotes relaxation.

Licorice Root: Supports hormonal balance with phytoestrogens that mimic estrogen.

Maca: Reduces symptoms related to hormonal imbalance during perimenopause.

Motherwort: Calming herb that reduces anxiety and promotes a sense of well-being.

Nettle Leaf: Reduces menstrual pain and alleviates symptoms of PMS.

Raspberry Leaf: Tones and strengthens the uterus and supports healthy menstrual cycles.

Red Clover: Alleviates menopausal symptoms such as hot flashes and night sweats.

Rose Petals: Tones and supports the health of the uterus, soothes and calms.

Sage: Reduces hot flashes, night sweats, and mood swings during perimenopause.

Shatavari: Supports hormonal balance and reproductive health.

St. John's Wort: Alleviates symptoms of mild to moderate depression and promotes a positive mood.

HERBAL TEA FOR SKIN AND HAIR

Two of the most visible representations of our health and well-being are our skin and hair. So, taking care of them is beneficial to looking and feeling our best. As we've already discovered, herbal teas have been used in many countries for centuries to promote overall health, and there is no exception when it comes to improving the health of our skin and hair.

Applied topically, the right blend of herbs can help nourish the skin, promote hair growth, and combat issues such as acne and dandruff. But in this chapter, we'll focus specifically on the benefits of ingesting these herbs in the form of herbal teas that can leave you looking and feeling radiant.

THE BENEFITS OF HERBS FOR SKIN AND HAIR HEALTH

Drinking herbal teas can lead to overall good health and well-being, which will result in healthy skin and hair. On the plus side, there are also specific herbs you can sip on that will improve the health of your skin and hair while benefiting the rest of you, too!

Herbal teas have been found to offer several benefits for skin and hair health due to their high concentration of antioxidants, vitamins, and minerals.

According to a study published in the Journal of Drugs in Dermatology, herbal teas can help improve skin health by reducing oxidative stress, inflammation, and collagen breakdown (Michalak, 2022). In addition, it has been suggested that herbal teas can help improve hair health by promoting hair growth, reducing hair loss, and improving scalp health (Park et al., 2021).

Some of the most beneficial herbs for skin and hair health include chamomile, peppermint, rosemary, lavender, horsetail, nettle leaf, green tea, and rooibos tea, but there are many more. Let's take a look at some recipes!

RECIPES FOR HERBAL TEAS THAT SUPPORT SKIN AND HAIR HEALTH

29. Nutrient-rich Hair Tea

Your ingredients:

- 1 tsp nettle leaf
- 1 tsp horsetail
- 1 bag of green tea
- 2 cups water

Tea Tip

All the tasty recipes in this chapter pull double duty. First, they will nourish your skin and hair from the inside out, so drink up!
Each also has topical applications for even more benefits.

The best way to make it:

1. In a pot, bring water to a boil.
2. Add the nettle leaf, horsetail, and green tea.
3. Allow them to steep for 5–10 minutes.
4. Strain and serve.

A snippet of insight into the ingredients:

Also known as stinging nettle, nettle leaf is full of Vitamins A, C, D, K, and B. It also contains amino acids, iron, potassium, silica, and sulfur, all of which strengthen hair and help it grow.

Horsetail, also known as equisetum, contains high amounts of silica, which helps your scalp create stronger hair.

In the context of hair growth, the EGCG in green tea stimulates hair growth, and as a DHT blocker, protects your hair follicles.

You can use nettle leaf, horsetail, and green tea topically as a rinse or mixed with a growth-stimulating essential oil as a scalp rub.

30. Circulation Boost Tea

Your ingredients:

- 1 tsp rosemary
- 1 tsp peppermint
- 1 tsp burdock root
- 2 cups water

The best way to make it:

1. In a pot, bring water to a boil.
2. Add the rosemary and burdock root.
3. Allow them to steep for 10 minutes.
4. Add the peppermint and steep for another 5 minutes.
5. Strain and serve.

A snippet of insight into the ingredients:

Rosemary, peppermint, and burdock root aid in healthy blood circulation, thus stimulating hair growth. In addition, burdock root is full of iron, potassium, and antioxidants.

Used topically, the tannins in burdock root tea help soothe an irritated or inflamed scalp, support healthy follicles, and reduce hair fall.

31. Healthy Hair Tea

Your ingredients:

- 1 tsp ginseng root
- 1 tsp hibiscus flower
- 1 tsp lavender
- 2 cups water

The best way to make it:

1. In a pot, bring water to a boil.
2. Add the ginseng, hibiscus flower, and lavender.

3. Allow them to steep for 10 minutes.
4. Strain and serve.

A snippet of insight into the ingredients:

Ginseng aids blood circulation, which, in turn, aids hair growth. It also helps strengthen hair so that it doesn't become brittle and break, and it assists in keeping hair follicles healthy.

Also known as *Hibiscus rosa-sinensis*, hibiscus is an edible plant. It is great at stimulating hair follicles for better growth and even increases the size of the hair follicle.

We have already discovered the calming benefits of lavender in previous recipes, but lavender has additional properties that make it great for hair health. In addition to drinking lavender in tea, lavender essential oils can soothe the scalp and get rid of bacterial and fungal infections.

32. Clear Skin Tea

Your ingredients:

- 1 tsp peppermint
- 1 tsp chamomile flower
- 1 tsp jasmine flower
- 2 cups water

The best way to make it:

1. In a pot, bring water to a boil.
2. Add the peppermint, chamomile, and jasmine flower.
3. Allow them to steep for 5–10 minutes.
4. Strain and serve.

A snippet of insight into the ingredients:

The menthol in peppermint can help improve hormonal imbalances and slow the production of excess sebum, so peppermint is helpful in preventing hormonal acne. Peppermint tea rids your skin of dead cells, which leaves your skin glowing.

Because chamomile is a stress reliever, it assists with all the things that allow your skin to look healthy—rest, better sleep, and less anxiety. Cooled chamomile tea, when applied directly to your skin, helps reduce puffiness around the eyes.

Jasmine's anti-inflammatory properties help soothe acne, remove blemishes and excess oils, and assist with anti-aging. Apply jasmine tea topically for quicker results.

33. Glowing Skin Tea

Your ingredients:

- 1 bag green tea
- 1 bag rooibos tea
- 1 tsp *Ginkgo biloba*
- 2 cups water

The best way to make it:

1. In a pot, bring water to a boil.
2. Add the tea bags and the *Ginkgo biloba.*
3. Allow them to steep for 10 minutes.
4. Strain and serve.

A snippet of insight into the ingredients:

Rooibos tea has high levels of antioxidants, alpha-hydroxy acids, and zinc. This tea helps protect against harmful free radicals and prevents fat loss under the skin, making it an almost magical anti-aging tea. Rooibos tea also has high levels of zinc, which can correct the hormone imbalances that trigger acne. Left to cool, rooibos tea can also be used as a facial rinse for all its topical benefits.

The anti-inflammatory properties of green tea mean that it's great for treating sensitive and acne-prone skin. The ECGC in green tea works from the inside to protect your skin against UV damage and the ani-oxidant reactivates dying skin cells.

Ginkgo biloba is full of antioxidants and works toward increasing blood circulation, both beneficial for healthy skin. When used topically, ginkgo's astringent properties can help shrink pores and reduce excess oil, while the antibacterial properties can prevent acne-causing bacteria.

34. Happy Hair and Healthy Skin Tea

Your ingredients:

- 1 tsp nettle leaf
- 1 tsp peppermint
- 1 tsp chamomile
- 1 bag green tea
- 2 cups water

The best way to make it:

1. In a pot, bring water to a boil.
2. Add the nettle leaf, chamomile, and green tea.
3. Allow them to steep for 5 minutes.
4. Add the peppermint and allow to steep for another 5 minutes.
5. Strain and serve.

A snippet of insight into the ingredients:

The combination of these ingredients offers not only skin and hair health as detailed in each recipe above, but also assists with overall health and well-being thanks to the presence of antioxidants and vitamins, and the calming properties of chamomile.

35. Nourishing Beau-Tea

Your ingredients:

- 1 tsp ginseng
- 1 tsp hibiscus flower
- 1 tsp jasmine flower
- 1 bag rooibos tea
- 2 cups water

The best way to make it:

1. In a pot, bring water to a boil.
2. Add the ginseng, hibiscus flower, jasmine, and rooibos.
3. Allow them to steep for 5–10 minutes.
4. Strain and serve.

A snippet of insight into the ingredients:

By combining these herbs, you're nourishing your skin, hair, and body. Every inch of you will benefit from the antioxidant-rich ingredients and the anti-aging properties of rooibos tea.

TIPS FOR INCORPORATING HERBAL TEAS INTO A NATURAL BEAUTY ROUTINE

Using herbal teas is a wonderful way to nourish your skin and hair from the inside out. Here are some tips to help you incorporate herbal teas into your natural beauty routine:

1. **Choose the right herbs.** As you've seen in this chapter, there are many herbs that are beneficial for the skin and hair. Each herb has its own unique benefits, so choose the ones that work best for your needs.

2. **Brew your tea.** To get the most benefit from your herbs, it's important to brew your tea correctly. The longer you steep your herbs, the more potent the tea will be.

3. **Use it as a toner.** Once your tea has cooled, you can use it as a facial toner. Apply the tea with a cotton ball or pad and let it dry. Herbal tea can soothe and calm your skin and reduce inflammation and redness.

4. **Add it to your bath.** You can also add your herbal tea to your bath for a relaxing and rejuvenating soak. The antioxidants and other beneficial compounds in the herbs will help to nourish your skin and leave you feeling refreshed. Imagine that, sipping on and soaking in herbal tea at the same time. Ah... bliss!

5. **Use it as a hair rinse.** After shampooing, rinse your hair with cooled herbal tea. This will help to condition and nourish your hair and scalp, leaving your hair soft and shiny and your follicles and scalp in great health.

By incorporating herbal teas into your beauty routine, you will enjoy the many health benefits of natural ingredients.

Bonus recipe: Herbal Hair Rinse

Your ingredients:

- 1 tsp aloe juice
- 1 tsp peppermint leaf
- 1 tsp hibiscus flower
- 1 tsp rosemary
- 1 tsp lavender
- 1 bag green tea

The best way to make it:

1. Boil 3 cups of water in a pot.
2. Add the peppermint, hibiscus, rosemary, lavender, and green tea.
3. Allow them to steep for 10–15 minutes.
4. Strain, allow to cool, and add the aloe juice.

A snippet of insight into the ingredients:

Aloe offers conditioning and stimulates hair growth. It is also wonderful for soothing the scalp.

Peppermint stimulates hair follicles for growth and leaves the scalp feeling clean and refreshed.

Hibiscus adds volume and shine and is great for conditioning.

Rosemary keeps hair shiny, strong, and healthy and promotes hair growth.

Lavender can be used to treat oily or dry hair because it balances the scalp's oil production. It stimulates circulation, resulting in healthy follicles, and is antibacterial.

Green tea is moisturizing, cleansing, and conditioning and adds smoothness.

Create Your Own Hair Rinse Recipe

In addition to the herbs listed in our recipe, you can mix and match any of the following herbal ingredients to make your own hair rinse following the method in our bonus recipe:

- Basil, to add shine while moisturizing and assisting growth. Nourishes hair and scalp.
- Bergamot, to revive hair bulbs to encourage hair growth. Contains stimulants that direct blood flow to the scalp, ensuring healthy delivery of nutrients and oxygen to the follicles.
- Burdock root, to assist with dry skin, scalp, and hair, dermatitis, and dandruff.
- Fenugreek is great for hair growth and conditioning, and it also keeps your scalp healthy.
- Ginseng, for hair growth and to treat baldness.
- Horsetail root is rich in selenium and silica, aiding hair growth and strengthening hair strands.
- Marshmallow makes a great moisturizer, conditioner, and detangler.
- Moringa is a natural conditioner.

- Nettle prevents hair loss, excessive oiliness, and dandruff.
- Oregano detangles and assists with scalp dryness and dandruff.
- Thyme, for oily hair and dandruff.

WRAPPING UP CHAPTER 6

There you go: another 7 recipes bringing us to a total of 35 thus far. Plus, we added that wonderful bonus recipe for a hair rinse! In the next chapter, we'll learn about 7 teas to relieve pain and inflammation.

CHAPTER 6 GLOSSARY

Basil: To add shine while moisturizing and assisting growth. Nourishes hair and scalp.

Bergamot: Revives hair bulbs to encourage hair growth. Contains stimulants that direct blood flow to the scalp, ensuring healthy delivery of nutrients and oxygen to the follicles.

Burdock Root: Rich in iron, potassium, and antioxidants, supports healthy hair and scalp.

Fenugreek: Great for hair growth and conditioning. Also keeps your scalp healthy.

Ginkgo Biloba: Increases blood circulation, beneficial for healthy skin and hair.

Ginseng: Improves blood circulation, strengthens hair, and promotes overall hair health.

Green Tea: Stimulates hair growth and protects against hair loss.

Hibiscus Flower: Stimulates hair follicles for better growth and increases the size of hair follicles.

Horsetail: High in silica, which helps create stronger hair and a healthy scalp.

Lavender: Soothes the scalp, helps with bacterial and fungal infections, and promotes hair health.

Marshmallow: Makes a great moisturizer, conditioner, and detangler.

Moringa: A natural conditioner.

Nettle Leaf: Contains vitamins and minerals that strengthen hair and promote growth.

Oregano: Detangles and assists with scalp dryness and dandruff.

Peppermint: Enhances blood circulation to the scalp, promoting hair growth.

Rooibos Tea: High in antioxidants, protects against free radicals, and helps correct hormone imbalances.

Rosemary: Aids in healthy blood circulation, stimulating hair growth.

Thyme: For oily hair and dandruff.

HERBAL TEA TO RELIEVE PAIN AND INFLAMMATION

One of the most noteworthy benefits of herbs is their ability to alleviate pain and inflammation in the body. Inflammation is the body's response to injury or infection, and while it is necessary for healing, prolonged inflammation can lead to chronic conditions such as arthritis, heart disease, and cancer. Plus, both pain and inflammation can be debilitating and significantly impact one's quality of life.

Fortunately, there are many herbs that possess anti-inflammatory and pain-relieving properties, and one of the most convenient and enjoyable ways to consume them is through herbal teas.

In this chapter, we will explore the different types of herbs that can help with pain and inflammation, how they work, and how to prepare them as teas. By the end of this chapter, you will have developed a better understanding of how these specific herbs and herbal teas can help you manage pain and inflammation naturally.

THE ANTI-INFLAMMATORY PROPERTIES OF HERBS

For centuries, herbs have been used for their medicinal properties, and their anti-inflammatory benefits are well-known.

Turmeric contains a powerful compound called curcumin, which has been found to possess anti-inflammatory properties. Turmeric has been used in traditional medicine to treat various inflammatory conditions (Prasad, 2011).

Another herb with anti-inflammatory properties is ginger. Ginger contains compounds called gingerols and shogaols. A study published in the Journal of Medicinal Food found that ginger supplementation can reduce the levels of inflammatory markers in the body, which may help relieve inflammation (Mashhadi et al., 2013).

Chamomile is also well-known for its anti-inflammatory properties. A study published in the Journal of Agricultural and Food Chemistry found that chamomile contains compounds called flavonoids that inhibit the production of inflammatory cytokines, thus alleviating pain and inflammation (Sah et al., 2022).

Incorporating herbs such as turmeric, ginger, chamomile, and the others we list in our recipes into your diet can help alleviate pain and inflammation. Let's start by looking at some recipes.

RECIPES FOR HERBAL TEAS TO RELIEVE PAIN AND INFLAMMATION

36. Pain Relief Tea

Your ingredients:

- 1 tsp ground turmeric
- 1/2 tsp ground ginger
- 2 cups water

The best way to make it:

1. In a pot, bring water to a boil.
2. Add the turmeric and ginger.
3. Allow them to simmer for 5–10 minutes.
4. Strain and serve.

A snippet of insight into the ingredients:

As described earlier, both turmeric and ginger have powerful anti-inflammatory properties. They can be used to assist with pain relief associated with arthritis, amongst other conditions.

37. Aches and Pains Away Tea

Your ingredients:

- 1–2 chamomile tea bags or 2 tsp chamomile flower
- 1 tsp ground cinnamon or a cinnamon stick
- 2 cups water

The best way to make it:

1. In a pot, bring water to a boil.
2. Add the chamomile and cinnamon.
3. Allow them to steep for 5–10 minutes.
4. Strain and serve.

A snippet of insight into the ingredients:

Chamomile has been found to have anti-inflammatory and analgesic properties that can help alleviate pain and inflammation.

Cinnamon is a powerful anti-inflammatory with potential for treating pain and the symptoms of rheumatoid arthritis. Cinnamon can increase blood circulation, which helps to relieve sore muscles and aching joints.

38. Pain and Inflammation Tea

Your ingredients:

- 1–2 green tea bags
- 1 tsp peppermint
- 2 cups water

The best way to make it:

1. In a pot, bring water to a boil.
2. Add the green tea and peppermint.
3. Allow them to steep for 5–10 minutes.
4. Strain and serve.

A snippet of insight into the ingredients:

Peppermint has been found to have anti-inflammatory and analgesic properties that can help alleviate pain and inflammation (Chumpitazi et al., 2018).

Amongst all its other health benefits, green tea is also able to fight inflammation and keep our joints healthy. It protects cartilage and encourages muscle repair. Some athletes use green tea as a sports supplement because of its role in reducing inflammation and muscle soreness (da Silva et al., 2018).

39. Natural Painkiller Tea

Your ingredients:

- 1–2 dried rose hips
- 1 tsp lemongrass
- 2 cups water

The best way to make it:

1. In a pot, bring water to a boil.
2. Add the rose hips and lemongrass.
3. Allow to simmer for 5–10 minutes.
4. Strain and serve.

Tea Tip

Lemongrass also pairs wonderfully with ginger for a tea remini-'scent' of Southeast Asia. More than that, these two herbs complement each other as anti-inflammatories and pain relievers.

A snippet of insight into the ingredients:

Rose hips are a rich source of vitamin C and have been found to have properties that can help alleviate pain and inflammation (Davidson, 2019).

The citral in lemongrass is a natural painkiller. Lemongrass helps to ease the joint pain associated with arthritis and has anti-inflammatory properties (Team, 2020).

40. Sweet Relief Tea

Your ingredients:

- 1 tablespoon meadowsweet leaf
- 1 tsp fennel
- 2 cups water

The best way to make it:

1. In a pot, bring water to a boil.
2. Add the meadowsweet and fennel.
3. Allow to steep for 5–10 minutes.
4. Strain and serve.

A snippet of insight into the ingredients:

Meadowsweet contains salicylates, which are natural compounds that have anti-inflammatory and pain-relieving properties (Streit, 2021).

Fennel is full of anti-inflammatory phenolic compounds like caffeoylquinic acid, rosmarinic acid, quercetin, and kaempferol (Sowbhagya, 2013).

41. Potent Pain Support Tea

Your ingredients:

- 1 tsp white willow bark
- 1 tsp nettle
- 2 cups water

The best way to make it:

1. In a pot, bring water to a boil.
2. Add the willow bark and nettle.
3. Allow to simmer for 5–10 minutes.
4. Strain and serve.

A snippet of insight into the ingredients:

White willow bark contains a compound called salicin, which is similar to aspirin and has anti-inflammatory and pain-relieving properties. This herb can help to relieve headaches, menstrual cramps, and other types of pain (University of Maryland Medical Center, n.d.).

Nettle leaf can be used to treat swelling and joint pain in conditions like arthritis (Raman, 2022).

Tea Tip

Our recipes serve as a guide. Depending on your specific pain and inflammation needs, you could blend variations of the ingredients featured in this chapter. For example, blend 1 tsp of cinnamon, or add peppermint or a bag of green tea to any of the other teas.

42. Arthritis Away Tea

Your ingredients:

- 1 tablespoon dried devil's claw root
- 1 tsp holy basil
- 2 cups water

The best way to make it:

1. In a pot, bring water to a boil.
2. Add the devil's claw and holy basil.
3. Allow to steep for 10–15 minutes.
4. Strain and serve.

A snippet of insight into the ingredients:

Devil's claw is a powerful anti-inflammatory herb that is commonly used to treat arthritis, back pain, and other types of pain and inflammation. This herb is best consumed on a regular basis for maximum benefit (Gxaba et al., 2022).

Compounds in the leaves and seeds of holy basil are believed to reduce levels of uric acid, alleviating the pain that results from inflammatory conditions like rheumatoid arthritis (Jamshidi et al., 2017).

TIPS FOR MANAGING CHRONIC PAIN WITH HERBAL TEAS

Living with chronic pain can be challenging, to say the least, but incorporating herbal teas into your daily routine can bring natural relief and improve your overall well-being. Here are some tips to help you effectively manage chronic pain with herbal teas:

1. **Experiment with different herbs.** Not all herbs are the same when it comes to pain relief. In the same way conventional medications have different uses, some herbs have specific properties that target inflammation, while others may target pain or help with relaxation and stress reduction. Try different herbs and combinations thereof to find the ones that work best for your specific type of pain.
2. **Choose high-quality herbs.** We have mentioned this before, but it is very important to opt for high-quality

herbs, not only for maximum effect, but also to protect yourself against the chemicals and pesticides found in low-grade teas. Look for organic, pesticide-free options to minimize the risk of potential contaminants.

3. **Brew properly.** The way you prepare your tea can impact its potency. Follow the instructions for brewing each herb carefully. Some herbs can be simmered while others must only be steeped, and then only for a time. Simmering and steeping the tea for the recommended time will allow for the optimal extraction of beneficial compounds.

4. **Consider herbal blends.** Blending herbs can create symbiotic effects and increase their individual properties. For example, ingesting black pepper with turmeric can increase the absorption of curcumin, the active compound in turmeric known for its anti-inflammatory properties (Goodson, 2018). For the most effective pain relief, explore different blends, bearing in mind our blending guidelines in Chapter 1, or consult with an herbalist to create personalized combinations that address your specific pain management needs.

5. **Stay consistent.** Herbal teas work best when consumed consistently over time, so rather than just 'trying' some from time to time, incorporate them into your daily routine to experience their long-term benefits. The compounds in herbal teas need time to build up in your system before you will feel their benefits, unlike conventional medication, which works quickly, but results in some undesirable side effects.

6. **Seek professional advice.** While herbal teas can be a valuable part of managing chronic pain, please seek guidance from a healthcare professional or herbalist. The right people can provide personalized recommendations based on your specific condition, medications, and any potential interactions. They will ensure that herbal teas complement your overall pain management plan safely and effectively.

Also, managing chronic pain is a holistic journey. Alongside herbal teas, consider incorporating other pain management strategies such as relaxation techniques, physical therapy, and other lifestyle adjustments that will optimize your well-being.

WRAPPING UP CHAPTER 7

There you go, another 7 recipes bringing us to a total of 42. We have covered a lot of ground. In Chapter 8, we'll learn about 7 teas for energy and focus.

CHAPTER 7 GLOSSARY

Chamomile: Has anti-inflammatory and analgesic properties.

Cinnamon: Possesses anti-inflammatory properties and aids in pain relief.

Devil's Claw: A powerful anti-inflammatory herb commonly used to treat pain and inflammation.

Fennel: Rich in anti-inflammatory phenolic compounds.

Ginger: Contains gingerols and shogaols, which help reduce inflammation.

Holy Basil: Helps reduce uric acid levels and alleviate pain in inflammatory conditions.

Lemongrass: Contains citral, a natural painkiller, and has anti-inflammatory properties.

Meadowsweet: Contains salicylates, providing anti-inflammatory and pain-relieving benefits.

Nettle Leaf: Used to treat swelling and joint pain, such as in arthritis.

Peppermint: Offers anti-inflammatory and analgesic effects.

Rose Hips: Rich in vitamin C and helps alleviate pain and inflammation.

Turmeric: Contains curcumin, which has anti-inflammatory properties.

White Willow Bark: Contains salicin, similar to aspirin, and has anti-inflammatory and pain-relieving properties.

8

HERBAL TEA FOR ENERGY AND FOCUS

We live in such a fast-paced world; maintaining energy and focus is essential for productivity and well-being. Coffee and energy drinks are one way to boost energy levels, but if you prefer natural alternatives that provide sustained vitality without unwanted side effects (think caffeine jitters or a sugar crash), consider herbal tea.

In this chapter, we explore herbal teas that can energize the body and enhance mental focus. From traditional herbs to unique blends, we uncover the power of nature's remedies to invigorate the body and mind.

Are you ready to awaken your senses, sharpen your focus, and experience sustained vitality? Well then, let's go—go—go!

THE ENERGIZING PROPERTIES OF HERBS

A variety of herbs possess energizing properties that will help to invigorate your body and enhance mental clarity:

For one, ginseng. Ginseng has been used for centuries in traditional Chinese medicine as an adaptogen, which means it helps the body adapt to stress and increase energy levels. Research suggests that ginseng may improve cognitive function, increase alertness, and reduce mental fatigue (Oliynyk, 2013).

Another herb known for its energizing effects is yerba mate. Yerba mate is derived from the leaves of the *Ilex paraguariensis* plant and is a popular beverage in South America. It contains natural compounds such as caffeine, theobromine, and theophylline, which contribute to its stimulating properties. Yerba mate is known to provide mental clarity, improve focus, and increase energy levels (Petre, 2023).

Other herbs like peppermint, rosemary, and ginger are also energizing. Peppermint offers a refreshing and uplifting aroma, while rosemary has been shown to enhance cognitive performance and mental alertness (Ghasemzadeh Rahbardar, 2020). Ginger can help improve circulation and, in so doing, promote energy.

By the end of this chapter, you will be able to create herbal tea blends that provide a natural pick-me-up, so say goodbye to energy slumps and say hello to sustained umph!

RECIPES FOR HERBAL TEAS THAT BOOST ENERGY AND IMPROVE FOCUS

43. Matcha Green Tea Boost

Your ingredients:

- 1 teaspoon matcha green tea powder
- 1 tsp – 1 tbsp coconut oil

Tea Tip

Traditionally, matcha green tea is made with water. But did you know you can make a matcha latte with steamed milk? Use whole, almond, coconut, or oat milk. Whisk till foamy, sweeten to taste, and enjoy.

How best to prepare

1. In a bowl, whisk the matcha green tea powder and coconut oil with a small amount of hot water to create a paste.

2. Gradually add the remaining hot water while whisking until the tea is frothy.

A snippet of insight into the ingredients:

Matcha green tea is rich in antioxidants and contains a natural source of caffeine, which can enhance alertness and concentration without the jitters (Ajmera, 2020).

Coconut oil is a healthy saturated fat that is known as a fuel for healthy brain function.

44. Energizing Green Tea Blend

Your ingredients:

- 1 bag green tea
- 1 tsp *Ginkgo biloba*
- 1 tsp lemon balm leaf or lemon zest
- 2 cups water

The best way to make it:

1. In a pot, bring water to a boil.
2. Add the green tea, ginkgo, and lemon balm leaf or lemon zest.
3. Allow to steep for 5 minutes.
4. Strain and serve.

A snippet of insight into the ingredients:

Green tea contains caffeine. It also contains an amino acid called L-theanine, which can promote focus (Mehta, 2021). The combination of caffeine and L-theanine helps improve alertness and concentration.

Ginkgo biloba has been studied for its ability to improve cognitive function, memory, and attention (Silberstein, 2011). This herb is believed to work by increasing blood flow and oxygen supply to the brain.

45. Revitalizing Tea Blend

Your ingredients:

- 1 tablespoon peppermint
- 1 tsp lemon balm leaf
- 1 tsp dry sage leaf or 4–5 fresh sage leaves
- 2 cups water

The best way to make it:

1. In a pot, bring water to a boil.
2. Add the peppermint, lemon balm leaf, and cinnamon.
3. Allow to steep for 5–10 minutes.
4. Strain and serve.

Tea Tip

Don't drink sage tea if you are pregnant. In fact, if you are pregnant or breast-feeding, consult a healthcare practitioner before consuming any herbal remedies.

A snippet of insight into the ingredients:

Peppermint has been shown to enhance cognitive performance and alertness (Moss et al., 2008), and lemon balm is believed to help promote a calm and focused state of mind (Cronkleton, 2019).

Sage is believed to improve alertness, attention, memory, mood, and overall cognitive function as well as reducing fatigue in adults (Kubala, 2020).

46. Enhancing Herbal Infusion

Your ingredients:

- 1 tablespoon dried gotu kola leaves
- 1 teaspoon dried lavender flower
- 1 tsp cinnamon or a cinnamon stick
- 2 cups water

The best way to make it:

1. In a pot, bring water to a boil.
2. Add the gotu kola, lavender, and cinnamon.
3. Allow to steep for 10 minutes.
4. Strain and serve.

A snippet of insight into the ingredients:

Gotu kola has been used in traditional medicine for its potential cognitive-enhancing properties. It is believed to work by enhancing cerebral blood flow and promoting neuroplasticity (Phoemsapthawee et al., 2022).

Lavender is known for its calming properties, but it can also have positive effects on focus and concentration because it promotes a relaxed yet focused state, allowing for improved concentration (Koulivand et al., 2013).

We have already discovered some of the benefits of cinnamon, but other studies have found that the scent of cinnamon boosts brain power to increase energy, focus, and alertness (Kawatra, 2015).

47. G^2 Vitali-Tea

Your ingredients:

- 1 teaspoon ginseng root powder
- 1 teaspoon fresh ginger root, grated or ground ginger
- 2 cups water

The best way to make it:

1. In a pot, bring water to a boil.
2. Add the ginseng and ginger.
3. Allow to steep for 5–10 minutes.
4. Strain and serve.

A snippet of insight into the ingredients:

Ginseng is known for its adaptogenic properties, which can help increase stamina and combat fatigue (Oliynyk, 2013).

Ginger is believed to enhance cognitive function and improve attention (Saenghong et al, 2012).

48. Holy Trini-Tea

Your ingredients:

- 1 tablespoon yerba mate leaf
- 1 tablespoon holy basil
- 1 teaspoon dried rosemary leaf
- 2 cups water

The best way to make it:

1. In a pot, bring water to a boil.
2. Add the yerba mate, holy basil, and rosemary.
3. Allow to steep for 5–10 minutes.
4. Strain and serve.

A snippet of insight into the ingredients:

As mentioned in the introduction to this chapter, the properties in yerba mate provide a stimulating effect on the central nervous system. This can lead to increased alertness and mental clarity.

As an adaptogenic herb, holy basil—also known as tulsi—can protect your body from stress and thus increase your energy levels.

Rosemary has been associated with cognitive benefits, including improved memory and concentration, and contains compounds that may enhance the activity of neurotransmitters involved in brain function (Ghasemzadeh Rahbardar, 2020).

49. Top Performance Tea

Your ingredients:

- 1 tsp maca root powder
- 1 tsp ashwagandha root powder or 1 tablespoon of dried ashwagandha root

The best way to make it:

1. In a pot, bring water to a boil.
2. Add maca root powder and ashwagandha.
3. Allow to simmer for 10–15 minutes.
4. Strain and serve.

A snippet of insight into the ingredients:

Maca root is believed to increase energy levels, stamina, and mental clarity (Kubala, 2022).

Ashwagandha has been associated with improved cognitive function, memory, and mental performance (Xing et al., 2022).

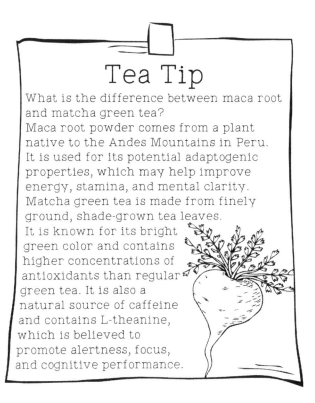

Tea Tip

What is the difference between maca root and matcha green tea?

Maca root powder comes from a plant native to the Andes Mountains in Peru. It is used for its potential adaptogenic properties, which may help improve energy, stamina, and mental clarity.

Matcha green tea is made from finely ground, shade-grown tea leaves. It is known for its bright green color and contains higher concentrations of antioxidants than regular green tea. It is also a natural source of caffeine and contains L-theanine, which is believed to promote alertness, focus, and cognitive performance.

TIPS FOR INCORPORATING HERBAL TEAS INTO YOUR PRODUCTIVITY ROUTINE

The right herbal teas can be a wonderful way to boost energy, enhance focus, and maintain mental clarity. Here are some tips to help you make the most of herbal teas in your productivity routine:

1. **Choose the right herbs.** Use herbs that are known for their energizing and focus-enhancing properties, like the ones we used in our recipes. These herbs can provide a natural energy boost without the jittery side

effects of more typical caffeine sources or the lousy sugar crash of energy drinks.

2. **Plan your tea breaks strategically.** Schedule specific times for tea breaks. Consider kickstarting your day with a cup of herbal tea and then enjoying another during the mid-afternoon slump to help you regain focus and energy. Experiment with what works best for your schedule and make your tea times a refreshing break.

3. **Let teatime be a grounding exercise.** If you are feeling anxious or, on the other hand, sleepy or lethargic, allow the preparation of herbal tea to shift your mindset. Focus on the tea-making steps: boiling the water, steeping the herbs, and savoring the aroma. Allow yourself a few minutes to relax. Take deep breaths while your tea brews. These purposeful actions can help you prepare for focused work ahead.

4. **Avoid excessive sugar or caffeine.** Herbal teas are a healthier alternative to sugary drinks or highly caffeinated beverages provided you don't add sugar. If you prefer a sweeter tea, choose natural sweeteners like honey or stevia. We will discuss various sweetener alternatives in our bonus chapter.

5. **Experiment with blends.** Experiment and mix different herbs to create tea blends that suit your taste preferences and specific energy and focus needs. Our recipes serve as a guide, and many of the herbs we use in this chapter can be mixed and matched.

6. **Stay hydrated.** Remember to stay properly hydrated as dehydration negatively affects productivity and

cognitive function. Herbal teas will contribute to your daily fluid intake, but it's important to drink plain water as well.

7. **Practice self-awareness.** Everyone's response to herbs will vary, so take note of how your body reacts to different teas. Remember to be patient as the effects of herbal remedies are not immediate.

Here's to a productive day with the power of herbal teas!

WRAPPING UP CHAPTER 8

That brings us to a total of 49 recipes! You're well on your way to having an herbal tea for every need, from aiding with digestive health and detoxification, immunity and stress relief, sleep and relaxation, healthy skin and hair, relief of pain and inflammation, and increased energy and focus. In the next chapter, we'll discover another 7 teas aimed at seasonal allergies.

CHAPTER 8 GLOSSARY

Ashwagandha: Improves cognitive function, memory, and mental performance.

Ginger: Enhances cognitive function and improves attention.

Ginseng: Adaptogenic herb that increases energy levels, improves cognitive function, and reduces mental fatigue.

Holy Basil: Adaptogenic herb that protects the body from stress and increases energy levels.

Maca Root: Increases energy levels, stamina, and mental clarity.

Peppermint: Enhances cognitive performance and alertness.

Rosemary: Enhances cognitive performance, memory, and mental alertness.

Yerba Mate: Contains caffeine, theobromine, and theophylline for mental clarity, improved focus, and increased energy levels.

HERBAL TEA FOR SEASONAL ALLERGIES

A rgh! —seasonal allergies! If you find yourself sniffling, sneezing, itching, and scratching your way through certain times of the year, this chapter is for you. Seasonal allergies—also referred to as hay fever or allergic rhinitis—affect millions of people worldwide. Rather than turning to over-the-counter and prescription medications, some people prefer natural remedies—cue herbal teas.

In this chapter, we will explore why certain herbs can alleviate your allergy symptoms and provide symptom-relieving herbal tea recipes for you to try. We hope you will experience first-hand how these brews can make a difference. So, whether you're a seasoned tea drinker or just testing the waters, get ready to discover how your next cuppa can be your ally when allergies make life uncomfortable.

THE ROLE OF HERBS IN REDUCING ALLERGIES

It's not uncommon for us to experience sniffling and sneezing noses or itchy and scratchy eyes during spring and fall. Perhaps you've wondered if antihistamine medication, nasal sprays, and eyedrops are the only way to combat these inescapable nemeses, especially considering the lousy side effects some of these conventional medications cause. The great news is that there is an alternative.

Research has shown that certain herbs can play a significant role in reducing seasonal allergies. For example, before you reach for the antihistamine, try some nettle tea. Nettle can act as a natural antihistamine, potentially reducing allergy symptoms (Roschek et al., 2009).

Another herb that has been traditionally used to combat allergies is butterbur. Research suggests that certain compounds in butterbur can block histamine receptors, which is how antihistamine drugs work (Gray, 2004).

Also, we've mentioned before that green tea is rich in a powerful antioxidant called EGCG. That means that green tea can help reduce the inflammation that often accompanies allergies (Maeda-Yamamoto, 2013).

Allergies occur when our immune system overreacts to an allergen, such as pollen or dust mites. In response to these allergens, our bodies produce histamine, a compound that leads to inflammation and the irritating symptoms we associate with allergies.

In addition, a healthy, strong immune system can help fight allergy symptoms. If your immune system is weak, the symptoms could last longer than usual. So ingesting herbs that boost your immune system will also help your body fight seasonal allergies.

While herbs and herbal teas won't cure your allergies, they can offer a natural way to soothe some of the symptoms. As always, consult with a healthcare provider before trying an alternative treatment, especially if you're currently taking medications or have any health conditions.

RECIPES FOR HERBAL TEAS THAT REDUCE ALLERGY SYMPTOMS

50. Combat Congestion Tea

Your ingredients:

- ½ cup fresh horehound leaves or ¼ cup dried leaves
- 1–2 teaspoons goldenrod leaves and young flowers
- 2 cups water

The best way to make it:

1. In a pot, bring water to a boil.
2. Add the horehound and goldenrod.
3. Allow to steep for 10 minutes.
4. Strain and serve.

A snippet of insight into the ingredients:

Horehound is a bitter member of the mint family. It is used to make cough drops, so you may have taken it in the past without even knowing. It helps thin and move mucus.

Goldenrod has three properties: antioxidant, anti-inflammatory, and antihistamine. Apart from combining well with horehound for a decongestant tea, it's also used as a kidney tonic (Got allergies, 2020).

Tea Tip

Not great for tea, but a great way to clear your sinuses, horseradish or wasabi can offer effective temporary relief, especially when prepared fresh.

51. Respiratory Relief Tea

Your ingredients:

- 1–2 teaspoons mullein leaf
- 1–2 teaspoons rosemary
- 1 teaspoon fresh lemon juice
- 2 cups water

The best way to make it:

1. In a pot, bring water to a boil.
2. Add the mullein leaf and rosemary.
3. Allow to steep for 10 minutes.
4. Strain, add the lemon juice, and serve.

Tea Tip

Adding fresh lemon or citrus juice to your allergy-relief teas will introduce vitamin C and help your body absorb the antioxidants found in many of the herbs that are used in these teas.

A snippet of insight into the ingredients:

Mullein leaf offers respiratory relief with healing properties that can soothe irritation and inflammation in the lungs.

Apart from its other medicinal uses, rosemary has recently been found to help relieve asthma symptoms thanks to the rosmarinic acid found in it. This acid has both anti-inflammatory and antioxidant properties (Got allergies, 2020).

52. Soothing Breath Tea

Your ingredients:

- 2–3 teaspoons nettle leaf
- 1–2 teaspoon mint
- 1–2 teaspoons holy basil
- 2 cups water

The best way to make it:

1. In a pot, bring water to a boil.
2. Add the nettle leaf, mint, and holy basil.
3. Allow to steep for 10 minutes.
4. Strain and serve.

A snippet of insight into the ingredients:

Studies have found that nettle is an effective natural treatment for respiratory allergies.

Not only is peppermint tea cooling, making it ideal for sore throats, but the peppermint scent helps unblock stuffy noses and eliminate sinus breath.

Holy basil can protect your body from stress and increase your energy levels when allergies get you down (Mona, 2021).

53. Green Tea with Ginger and Lemon Grass*
a spin on the old lemon and ginger classic

Your ingredients:

- 1 bag green tea
- 1-inch fresh ginger root, sliced
- 1 teaspoon lemongrass
- 2 cups water

Tea Tip

Goji berry tea pairs well with ginger and is soothing to the digestive system.

The best way to make it:

1. In a pot, bring water to a boil.
2. Add the green tea, ginger, and lemongrass.
3. Allow to steep for 10 minutes.
4. Strain and serve.

A snippet of insight into the ingredients:

We have covered the anti-inflammatory properties of green tea before, so you will know by now that an herbal tea blend with green tea is great for your overall well-being. In addition, it has been found that green tea can reduce the symptoms of seasonal allergies.

Ginger will not only treat the nausea you may experience as a result of an allergy-related postnasal drip, but it can also help lessen the symptoms of sinusitis (Mona, 2021).

Lemongrass is naturally uplifting and gives your immune system a boost. It is loaded with antioxidants and is high in vitamins C and A (Team, 2020).

54. Therapeutic Tea

Your ingredients:

- 1 bag rooibos tea
- 1–2 teaspoons echinacea
- 1–2 teaspoon elderberry
- 2 cups water

The best way to make it:

1. In a pot, bring water to a boil.
2. Add the rooibos tea, echinacea, and elderberry.
3. Allow to steep for 10 minutes.
4. Strain and serve.

A snippet of insight into the ingredients:

Previously we discovered how good rooibos tea is for your digestion, skin, and hair. Now, we can confirm that the antioxidants in rooibos, which can lead to overall well-being, make it a great tea to use in therapeutic blends.

Echinacea is known to support the immune system and fight off infection.

Elderberries are high in antioxidants, have antiviral properties, and help reduce the symptoms of allergies, colds, and flu (Sipsby, n.d.).

55. High C Tea

Your ingredients:

- 1–2 teaspoons dried goji
- 1–2 teaspoons moringa
- 1–2 teaspoon hibiscus
- 2 cups water

The best way to make it:

1. In a pot, bring water to a boil.
2. Add the goji, moringa, and hibiscus.
3. Allow to steep for 5–10 minutes.
4. Strain and serve.

A snippet of insight into the ingredients:

Goji berries contain Vitamin C and A to support your immune system. They're a great source of zinc, one of the nutrients that can help you fight off symptoms of allergies, colds, and flu.

Moringa contains immune boosting nutrients. It acts as a natural antibacterial and antifungal too.

Hibiscus is loaded with vitamin C and tastes delicious with its naturally sweet and tart infusion. It is frequently used to ease sore throats because it's so high in antioxidants (Sipsby, n.d.).

56. Regulate Immuni-Tea

Your ingredients:

- 1 teaspoon dried licorice root
- 1–2 teaspoons turmeric
- 1–2 teaspoon yerba mate leaf
- 2 cups water

The best way to make it:

1. In a pot, bring water to a boil.
2. Add the licorice, turmeric, and yerba mate.
3. Allow to steep for 5–10 minutes.
4. Strain and serve.

A snippet of insight into the ingredients:

Licorice root is known to support immune function and has anti-inflammatory properties (Wahab et al., 2021).

Turmeric features in a lot of places throughout this book. Its natural healing properties make it one of our all-star players. In the context of allergy relief, turmeric helps regulate the immune system, protecting your body against allergies, particularly by reducing the irritation and swelling caused by allergic rhinitis (Mona, 2021).

Yerba mate contains natural anti-inflammatory properties, vitamins C and E, selenium, and zinc—nutrients that may help boost your immune system and therefore help you overcome those allergy symptoms (Mona, 2021).

TIPS FOR MANAGING SEASONAL ALLERGIES WITH HERBAL TEAS

A comforting cup of herbal tea could be just the natural remedy you need to alleviate pesky allergy symptoms. Isn't it great to know that you can use herbal teas to navigate your way through the allergy season? Let's explore some tips to get you started:

1. **Experiment with different herbs.** Not all herbs are created equal when it comes to allergy relief. Some herbs have properties that help reduce inflammation, others may help with congestion or sinus relief, while some promote overall relaxation and wellness. Experiment with different flavors and monitor the outcomes to see which herbs soothe your allergic symptoms the best.

2. **Choose high-quality herbs.** This point can't be emphasized enough—the quality of the herbs you choose can directly impact their effectiveness. So be sure to choose organic, pesticide-free options. Doing so will ensure you're benefiting from the best possible therapeutic effects without consuming potential contaminants.

3. **Brew properly.** Following the correct brewing instructions for each herb will allow for optimal extraction of the beneficial compounds. Some herbal extracts can be simmered, but others must only be steeped. Some become bitter if left for too long, while others may lose some of their health benefits. Always follow the directions provided.

4. **Benefit from blends.** Blending herbs can amplify their properties, providing more comprehensive relief. The herbs listed in all our recipes can be consumed as single-ingredient teas, but blends offer more benefits, can be more effective, or simply offer more enjoyable

flavor profiles. To be safe, refer to our blending guidelines in Chapter 1, or consult with a professional herbalist to create personalized blends that address your specific allergy needs.

5. **Stay consistent.** To experience the full potential of herbal teas, incorporate them into your daily routine throughout allergy season as they offer the most benefit when consumed consistently. It may take some time for the beneficial compounds in the tea to build up in your system and provide noticeable relief, so be patient.

6. **Seek professional advice.** Although herbal teas are a great way to treat seasonal allergies, it's always best to consult a healthcare professional or herbalist. While none of the herbs mentioned in these recipes is harmful on its own, a professional will provide personalized advice based on your specific allergies, including any potential interactions with medications you might be taking.

Now, enjoy your tea and enjoy being sneeze-free!

WRAPPING UP CHAPTER 9

There you have it, another chapter, another 7 teas. That brings us to a total of 56 herbal teas. Next up, we're going to look at 7 herbal teas for athletic performance.

CHAPTER 9 GLOSSARY

Echinacea: Supports the immune system and fights off infections.

Elderberry: High in antioxidants, and antiviral properties, helps reduce allergy, cold, and flu symptoms.

Ginger: Treats nausea and lessens symptoms of sinusitis.

Goji Berries: Supports the immune system, high in Vitamin C, A, and zinc.

Goldenrod: Acts as an antioxidant, anti-inflammatory, and antihistamine, aiding in decongestion and serving as a kidney tonic.

Green Tea: Reduces inflammation, including allergy-related inflammation.

Hibiscus: High in vitamin C, eases sore throats, and is rich in antioxidants.

Holy Basil: Protects the body from stress and increases energy levels during allergies.

Horehound: Thins and moves mucus and provides respiratory relief.

Lemongrass: Uplifting, boosts the immune system, high in antioxidants, vitamins C and A.

Licorice Root: Supports immune function and has anti-inflammatory properties.

Moringa: Contains immune-boosting nutrients and acts as a natural antibacterial and antifungal.

Mullein Leaf: Soothes irritation and inflammation in the lungs.

Nettle: Acts as a natural antihistamine, reducing allergy symptoms.

Peppermint: Cooling, ideal for sore throats, unblocks stuffy noses, and eliminates sinus breath.

Rooibos: Contains antioxidants for overall well-being.

Rosemary: Contains rosmarinic acid, which has anti-inflammatory and antioxidant properties and helps relieve asthma symptoms.

Turmeric: Regulates the immune system, reduces irritation and swelling caused by allergic rhinitis.

Yerba Mate: Contains natural anti-inflammatory properties, boosts the immune system with vitamins C and E, selenium, and zinc.

HERBAL TEA FOR ATHLETIC PERFORMANCE

Athletic performance comprises optimal physical conditioning, mental focus, and efficient recovery. Well-being, nutrition, and recovery are the pillars of athletic success. Many athletes look for ways to enhance their performance and gain a competitive edge.

In this chapter, we investigate the world of herbal teas and their potential to enhance athletic performance. Herbs offer a natural and holistic approach to supporting the body and mind during intense physical activity. Packed with bioactive compounds, herbal teas can provide valuable support in areas like focus, energy, endurance, recovery, and stress adaptation.

Herbal teas are not magic potions that guarantee instant athletic success; rather, they should be used in parallel with a holistic approach to training and overall well-being. A healthy combination of proper training, adequate nutrition, restful sleep, and smart supplementation—including herbal teas—can contribute to unlocking your full potential as an athlete.

While herbal teas have been used for their potential benefits in athletic performance, please consult with a healthcare professional, sports nutritionist, or herbalist before incorporating herbal teas into your routine, especially if you have specific health conditions or are taking medications that may interact with certain herbs.

THE BENEFITS OF HERBS FOR ATHLETIC PERFORMANCE

Combined with proper nutrition and training, herbs can aid athletic performance because they contain natural compounds and properties that support athletes in achieving their goals. Let's explore some of the key benefits of herbs for athletic performance.

Enhanced endurance

Certain herbs are believed to improve endurance, allowing athletes to sustain physical activity for longer. For example, *Rhodiola rosea*—commonly known as rhodiola and "golden root" —has adaptogenic properties that help the body adapt to stress and increase endurance capacity (van de Walle, 2023). Not strictly an herb, but a well-known medicinal, cordyceps fungus has been found to enhance oxygen utilization and thereby improve endurance (Liu et al., 2015).

Increased energy and focus

Maintaining optimal energy levels and mental focus is essential for athletes. Herbs like ginseng and maca root have been traditionally used to enhance energy, stamina, and mental clarity (Kubala, 2020).

Reduced inflammation and muscle recovery

Athletic exertion can lead to inflammation and muscle damage, most commonly felt as muscle stiffness. Herbs such as turmeric and ginger possess anti-inflammatory properties that can help athletes bounce back quicker after strenuous workouts or competitions (Raman, 2023).

Improved stress adaptation

During training and competitions, athletes face physical and mental stress, which can impact their performance. Adaptogenic herbs like ashwagandha and holy basil help the body adapt to stress, enhancing resilience and overall performance (Chandrasekhar et al., 2012).

Muscle strength and power

Some herbs have been found to benefit muscle strength and power. *Tribulus terrestris* (TT)—also known as puncture vine and gokshura—has been traditionally used to support and promote athletic performance (Pokrywka, 2014).

Next up, we will explore 7 herbal tea recipes that can support athletic performance. By incorporating them into your existing training routine, you can harness their potential benefits to optimize your performance.

RECIPES FOR HERBAL TEAS THAT BOOST ENDURANCE AND REDUCE RECOVERY TIME

57. Matcha Green Tea

Your ingredients:

- 1 tsp matcha green tea

The best way to make it:

1. Add matcha green tea powder to a cup.
2. Pour hot water into the cup.
3. Whisk vigorously until the tea is frothy.
4. Enjoy before or after workouts for an energy boost.

A snippet of insight into the ingredients:

Matcha green tea is rich in antioxidants and contains caffeine, which can improve alertness, focus, and physical performance (Pervin et al., 2018).

58. Power Boost Tea

Your ingredients:

- 1 small beetroot, peeled and chopped
- 1-inch fresh ginger sliced, or 1 tsp dried powdered ginger
- 2 cups water

The best way to make it:

1. In a pot, bring water to a boil.
2. Add the beetroot and ginger.
3. Allow to simmer for 10 minutes.
4. Strain and serve.
5. Enjoy as a pre- or post-workout drink.

A snippet of insight into the ingredients:

Beetroot is known to improve performance as it contains nitrates that can enhance blood flow and oxygen delivery to muscles (Murphy, 2012).

Ginger, as we have already discovered, has anti-inflammatory properties and can aid in post-workout recovery.

59. Refresh and Alert Tea

Your ingredients:

- 1 bag green tea or 1 tsp green tea leaves
- 1 tsp ginseng powder or sliced ginseng root
- Juice from half a lemon
- 2 cups water

The best way to make it:

1. In a pot, bring water to a boil.
2. Add the green tea and ginseng.
3. Allow to steep for 5–10 minutes.
4. Strain, add the lemon juice, and serve.
5. Enjoy before workouts for increased energy and focus.

A snippet of insight into the ingredients:

As we have already discovered, ginseng is known to enhance endurance, reduce fatigue, and improve cognitive function, making it beneficial for athletic performance.

Green tea contains catechins and caffeine, which can enhance fat oxidation and promote alertness during exercise (Venables et al., 2008).

Finally, lemon juice provides a refreshing flavor, and can aid in hydration.

60. Level Up Tea

Your ingredients:

- 1–2 tsp cinnamon
- 1–2 tsp turmeric
- ¼ tsp black pepper
- 2 cups water

The best way to make it:

1. In a pot, bring water to a boil.
2. Add the cinnamon, turmeric, and black pepper.
3. Stir well until fully combined.
4. Enjoy post-workout to reduce inflammation and support recovery.

A snippet of insight into the ingredients:

Although we've learned a lot about cinnamon already, in this context it has been associated with improved exercise performance by increasing glucose uptake and reducing inflammation.

We have also already made the acquaintance of curcumin, the compound in turmeric known for its anti-inflammatory and antioxidant properties. And we learned that black pepper enhances the absorption of curcumin in the body, maximizing its benefits.

61. Happy Heart Tea

Your ingredients:

- 1 bag rooibos tea or 1 tsp tea leaves
- 1–2 tsp hibiscus flower
- 2 cups water

The best way to make it:

1. In a pot, bring water to a boil.
2. Add the rooibos tea and hibiscus flower.
3. Allow to steep for 5–10 minutes.
4. Strain and serve.
5. Enjoy as a refreshing pre- or post-workout drink.

A snippet of insight into the ingredients:

Rooibos tea is rich in antioxidants and may help improve exercise performance by reducing oxidative stress and inflammation (Joubert et al., 2008), and hibiscus has been associated with enhanced endurance and cardiovascular health (Abubakar et al., 2019).

62. High Endurance Tea

Your ingredients:

- 1 tsp ginseng
- 1 tsp rhodiola
- 1 tsp ashwagandha
- 2 cups water

The best way to make it:

1. In a pot, bring water to a boil.
2. Add ginseng, rhodiola, and ashwagandha.
3. Allow to steep for 5–10 minutes.
4. Strain and serve.
5. Enjoy before your workout.

A snippet of insight into the ingredients:

You are now familiar with the wonders of ginseng, and we mentioned rhodiola in this chapter's intro. Rhodiola especially good for workouts that include weightlifting, HIIT, or other strength training, as it boosts anaerobic performance.

Ashwagandha is another herb that features throughout this book but, in this context, it will increase your aerobic endurance, allowing you to get the most from your workout (Jacob, 2023).

63. Energy Enhance Tea

Your ingredients:

- 1 tsp oolong tea leaves
- 5–6 fresh mint leaves
- Zest from 1 orange
- 2 cups water

The best way to make it:

1. In a pot, bring water to a boil.
2. Add the oolong tea, mint, and orange zest.
3. Allow to steep for 5 minutes.
4. Strain and serve.
5. Enjoy before or after your workout.

A snippet of insight into the ingredients:

Oolong tea contains caffeine and polyphenols that can enhance alertness and support metabolism during physical activity (Zang et al., 2020).

We have already learned that mint is a cooling tea that can aid digestion, and orange zest provides a refreshing citrus flavor and contains vitamin C, which supports immune health.

Tea Tip

Turn any herbal tea into a nutrient-packed, energizing smoothie by blending cooled or iced tea with some of your favorite fruits! We'll discover more about this in the bonus chapter.

TIPS FOR INCORPORATING HERBAL TEAS INTO A FITNESS ROUTINE

Herbal teas can be a wonderful addition to your fitness routine, providing hydration with numerous potential health benefits. Here are some tips to help you incorporate them:

1. **Choose refreshing and hydrating blends.** Opt for herbal teas that contain peppermint, lemongrass, and hibiscus; they can replenish fluids and quench your thirst during and after workouts.
2. **Enjoy pre-workout boosters.** Certain herbs can provide a natural energy boost and enhance focus before a workout. Teas containing ingredients like green tea, ginseng, or yerba mate have the potential to improve energy levels and mental alertness.

3. **Support recovery with anti-inflammatory herbs.**
   After an intense workout, herbal teas with anti-
   inflammatory properties can aid in muscle recovery
   and reduce post-exercise inflammation. Turmeric,
   ginger, and boswellia are the best options for faster
   recovery.

4. **Incorporate adaptogenic herbs.** Including adaptogenic
   herbs like ashwagandha, rhodiola, or holy basil in your
   herbal tea blends can help improve resilience and aid
   overall recovery.

5. **Experiment with blends and combinations.** Get
   creative and blend different herbs to create your own
   unique teas. Just be sure to refer to our blending guide
   in Chapter 1.

6. **Consider timing and dosage.** Some teas have
   stimulating effects, so it's best not to drink them too
   close to bedtime. In our recipes, we noted whether the
   teas are best enjoyed before or after your workout.
   Always be mindful of the dosage recommendations.

7. **Prioritize quality and sourcing.** Choose high-quality
   herbal teas from reputable sources to ensure purity,
   potency, and safety. Where possible, opt for organic
   ingredients to minimize your exposure to pesticides
   and other contaminants.

8. **Listen to your body.** Your body is unique, so pay
   attention to how herbal teas make you feel. If you
   experience any adverse reactions or sensitivities,
   discontinue, and consult with a healthcare professional.

Most notable, herbal teas are not a substitute for a balanced diet, regular exercise, and professional medical advice. Rather, they can be a healthy and natural supportive addition to your fitness routine.

WRAPPING UP CHAPTER 10

We now have 63 recipes in our herbal tea box. Up next, our final chapter with 7 teas for brain health, and then we have our bonus chapter!

CHAPTER 10 GLOSSARY

Ashwagandha: Increases aerobic endurance and allows for optimal workout performance.

Beetroot: Contains nitrates that enhance blood flow and oxygen delivery to muscles.

Black Pepper: Enhances the absorption of curcumin in the body.

Cinnamon: Improves exercise performance by increasing glucose uptake and reducing inflammation.

Ginger: Anti-inflammatory properties, aids in post-workout recovery.

Ginseng: Enhances endurance, reduces fatigue, and improves cognitive function.

Green Tea: Contains catechins and caffeine, enhances fat oxidation, and promotes alertness during exercise.

Hibiscus: Enhances endurance and cardiovascular health.

Matcha Green Tea: Rich in antioxidants and contains caffeine, improves alertness, focus, and physical performance.

Mint: Cooling, aids digestion.

Oolong Tea: Contains caffeine and polyphenols, enhances alertness, and supports metabolism during physical activity.

Rhodiola: Boosts anaerobic performance, suitable for strength training.

Rooibos Tea: Rich in antioxidants, reduces oxidative stress and inflammation, and improves exercise performance.

Turmeric: Anti-inflammatory and antioxidant properties.

HERBAL TEA FOR BRAIN HEALTH

Our brain plays a crucial role in keeping us alive and well, yet we often forget to care for it as much as we care for other parts of our body. In truth, our brain requires proper care, hydration, and nourishment to function optimally. Various vitamins, minerals and supplements have the necessary properties to feed our brain, but did you know some herbs and other natural ingredients (including some spices and a few mushrooms) have properties that can aid in brain health?

Herbal teas have been used for centuries to support brain health and enhance cognitive function. Packed with a variety of beneficial compounds, these teas can boost mental clarity, focus, and overall brain performance—from improving memory and concentration to reducing mental fatigue and supporting neuroprotective mechanisms.

In this chapter, we will delve into the fascinating world of herbal teas for brain health. Don't be too surprised when you see spices and mushrooms making their way into the recipes—they're all so good for you!

THE BENEFITS OF HERBS FOR BRAIN HEALTH

When it comes to maintaining optimal brain health, nature can play a valuable role. Many botanicals and fungi—including herbs, spices, and mushrooms—contain bioactive compounds that have been found to improve cognitive function, slow down brain aging, and enhance memory, focus, and overall brain health. Let's explore some of the remarkable benefits that brain-boosting botanicals and fungi can offer.

Enhancing cognitive function

Studies have found that certain herbs have the potential to support cognitive function and mental clarity. For example, *Ginkgo biloba*, *Bacopa monnieri*, and rosemary have been traditionally used to improve memory, attention, and concentration (Spencer et al., 2017). How do they work? These herbs contain compounds that may enhance blood flow to the brain, promote neuroprotective effects, and support neurotransmitter activity.

Boosting mood and emotional well-being

Our mental well-being is closely linked to brain health. Herbs like St. John's wort and lemon balm have been traditionally used relieve symptoms of mild depression and anxiety (Lui et al., 2015), providing a natural support for emotional well-being, which is one part of brain health.

Protecting against age-related cognitive decline

As we get older, it becomes increasingly important to support brain health and preserve cognitive function. Certain herbs have shown promise in protecting against age-related cognitive decline. The curcumin in turmeric exhibits antioxidant and anti-inflammatory properties that may help combat oxidative stress and inflammation in the brain (Mishra et al., 2008).

Supporting neuroplasticity

Neuroplasticity is the brain's ability to change, adapt, and form new connections. Ingredients like gotu kola and lion's mane mushroom are associated with potential benefits for neuroplasticity (Kidd, 2005). These may support the growth and development of brain cells, promoting overall brain health and function.

Reducing oxidative stress and inflammation

Chronic inflammation and oxidative stress are known to contribute to various neurological conditions and cognitive decline. Herbs such as ginger, green tea, and ashwagandha contain potent antioxidants and anti-inflammatory compounds that can help reduce oxidative damage and inflammation in the brain (Singh, 2011).

While herbs, spices, and mushrooms have shown promise in supporting brain health, they should not replace medical advice or treatment. If you have specific concerns about brain health or cognitive function, it's always best to consult with a health-care professional.

Now, grab your favorite cuppa and let's see what brain boosting teas we have concocted.

RECIPES FOR HERBAL TEAS THAT PROMOTE BRAIN HEALTH

64. Brain Protect Tea

Your ingredients:

- 1–2 tsp nutmeg
- 1-inch fresh ginger sliced, or 1 tsp dried powdered ginger
- 1–2 tsp saffron
- 2 cups water

The best way to make it:

1. In a pot, bring water to a boil.
2. Add the nutmeg, ginger, and saffron.
3. Allow to steep for 10 minutes.
4. Strain and serve.

A snippet of insight into the ingredients:

Nutmeg contains myristicin, a compound that helps prevent the formation of beta-amyloid plaques, which are the plaques seen in Alzheimer's disease.

Ginger has the potential to reduce the oxidative stress that causes brain cells to age and die, and it protects against neurodegenerative diseases (Mirmosayyeb et al., 2017).

In traditional medicine, saffron is used to support brain, liver, and lung function. Current research suggests that saffron aids in memory support and brain health, specifically, its ability to support brain aging, focus, and mood. Studies also suggest that saffron can support learning and memory (Jackson et al., 2021).

65. Sharp Mind Tea

Your ingredients:

- 1–2 sticks of cinnamon or 1–2 tsp dried cinnamon
- 1–2 tsp dried sage
- 5–6 fresh peppermint leaves or 1–2 tsp dried peppermint
- 2 cups water

The best way to make it:

1. In a pot, bring water to a boil.
2. Add the cinnamon, sage, and peppermint.
3. Allow to steep for 5–10 minutes.

4. Strain and serve.

A snippet of insight into the ingredients:

Studies suggest that cinnamon and its active compounds—including cinnamaldehyde, coumarin, and tannins—can improve brain health, reduce oxidative stress or inflammation, and possibly prevent dementia (Forbes, 2023).

Sage may improve cognition and aid in the treatment of Alzheimer's disease. A research review suggests that sage contains compounds that may be beneficial for cognitive and neurological function (Wong, 2023)

Peppermint has been shown to enhance cognitive function, boosting recall and sharpening your mind (Wack, 2022).

66. *Bacopa monnieri* and Rosemary tea

Your ingredients:

- 1–2 tsp *Bacopa monnieri* powder
- 5–6 sprigs of fresh rosemary or 1–2 tsp dried rosemary
- 2 cups water

The best way to make it:

1. In a pot, bring water to a boil.
2. Add the *Bacopa monnieri* and rosemary.
3. Allow to steep for 5–10 minutes.
4. Strain and serve.

A snippet of insight into the ingredients:

Also known as brahmi and water hyssop, *Bacopa monnieri* is an herb that contains powerful anti-inflammatory and cognition-enhancing properties.

Rosemary contains a neuroprotective compound known as carnosic acid, which can protect the brain from free radical damage (Naturopathic, 2022).

67. Brain Repair Tea

Your ingredients:

- 1–2 tsp gotu kola
- 1–2 tsp lemon balm
- 1 bag green tea
- 2 cups water

The best way to make it:

1. In a pot, bring water to a boil.
2. Add the gotu kola, lemon balm, and green tea.
3. Allow to steep for 5 minutes.
4. Strain and serve.

A snippet of insight into the ingredients:

In preliminary studies, tests demonstrated that gotu kola may inhibit Alzheimer's-associated oxidative stress and improve cognitive function. Another study found that patients with mild to moderate Alzheimer's disease who took lemon balm extract had a greater improvement in cognitive function compared to those given a placebo (Wong, 2023).

The antioxidants and anti-inflammatory compounds found in green tea can help reduce oxidative damage and inflammation in the brain (Singh, 2011).

68. Memory Protect Tea

Your ingredients:

- 1–2 tsp dried ashwagandha root
- 1–2 tsp dried ginseng root
- 2 cups water

The best way to make it:

1. In a pot, bring water to a boil.
2. Add the ashwagandha and ginseng.
3. Allow to steep for 5–10 minutes.
4. Strain and serve.

A snippet of insight into the ingredients:

Ashwagandha has been found to inhibit the formation of beta-amyloid plaques in preliminary research, and studies have indicated that ashwagandha may benefit the brain by reducing oxidative stress, which is associated with Alzheimer's disease.

Ginseng has the potential to prevent memory loss and reduce age-related memory decline (Wong, 2023).

69. Circulate and Protect Tea

Your ingredients:

- 1–2 tsp turmeric
- 1–2 tsp *Ginkgo biloba*
- 2 cups water

The best way to make it:

1. In a pot, bring water to a boil.
2. Add the turmeric and ginkgo.
3. Allow to steep for 10 minutes.
4. Strain and serve.

A snippet of insight into the ingredients:

We've learned so much about the benefits of curcumin already. In the context of brain health, the curcumin found in turmeric may boost brain health and stave off Alzheimer's disease by clearing the brain of beta-amyloid, a protein fragment known to form Alzheimer's-related brain plaques.

Ginkgo biloba is a commonly taken dementia remedy in traditional Chinese medicine. *Ginkgo biloba* may improve cognitive function by stimulating circulation and promoting blood flow to the brain (Wong, 2023).

70. Mushroom Blend Tea

Your ingredients:

- Lion's mane mushroom tea powder, and/or
- Reishi mushroom tea powder, and/or
- Chaga mushroom tea powder

The best way to make it:

The best way to make mushroom tea is to soak mushrooms in boiling hot water because it breaks down the cell walls of the mushrooms, making their nutrients easier to absorb. Drinking mushroom tea is an effective and enjoyable way to absorb their many health benefits. Our recipe is based on store-bought mushroom tea powders. We recommend following the brand-specific directions.

A snippet of insight into the ingredients:

Three of the most well-known medicinal mushrooms are lion's mane, reishi, and chaga. They all have high concentrations of vitamins, nutrients, and antioxidants and can support digestion, energy, mental clarity, mood, relaxation and sleep, the immune system and brain health (Tamim Teas 2021).

Lion's mane offers a brain boost. One study found that lion's mane has the potential to enhance memory, focus, and cognition. Another correlates the use of lion's mane to neurogenesis (Mori et al., 2009). Lion's mane tea is mild and slightly sweet.

Reishi are nicknamed the mushroom of immortality. It is comparable to turmeric and other natural anti-inflammatories. Studies suggest reishi can aid with immune support, improved circulation, and mood elevation. These in turn lead to a healthier brain (Stieg, 2018). Reishi tea tastes earthy, woody, and slightly bitter.

Chaga is the most antioxidant-rich medicinal mushroom. Chaga contains B-complex vitamins, vitamin D, cesium, amino acids, iron, selenium, calcium, copper, magnesium, manganese, potassium, rubidium, fiber, and zinc which have been linked to brain health (Elay, 2011). Chaga tea tastes earthy and slightly bitter.

Although they can be enjoyed separately, we recommend a combination of lion's mane, reishi, and chaga for brain health and overall well-being (Tamim Teas, 2021).

Mushroom tea is adaptogenic and can be safely blended with any adaptogen such as ashwagandha, rhodiola, ginseng, holy basil, licorice, maca, and cordyceps. It is also safe to blend mushroom tea with peppermint, lemon balm, ginger, chamomile, cinnamon, rosemary, and green tea.

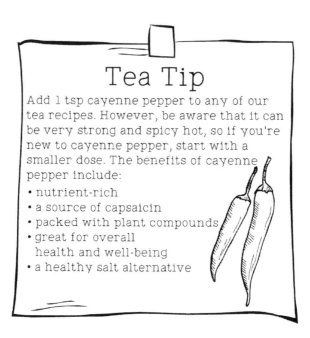

Tea Tip

Add 1 tsp cayenne pepper to any of our tea recipes. However, be aware that it can be very strong and spicy hot, so if you're new to cayenne pepper, start with a smaller dose. The benefits of cayenne pepper include:

- nutrient-rich
- a source of capsaicin
- packed with plant compounds
- great for overall
  health and well-being
- a healthy salt alternative

TIPS FOR INCORPORATING HERBAL TEAS INTO YOUR BRAIN HEALTH ROUTINE

Incorporating herbal teas into your brain health routine is the best way to support cognitive function and overall brain well-being. Here are some tips to help you make the most of herbal teas for brain health:

1. **Choose brain-boosting herbs.** Look for ingredients known for their cognitive-enhancing properties, such as *Ginkgo biloba*, rosemary, gotu kola, *Bacopa monnieri*, and lion's mane.
2. **Create a daily tea ritual.** Make herbal tea a part of your daily routine. Set aside a dedicated time each day to brew and enjoy a cup of brain-boosting herbal tea.

3. **Opt for organic and high-quality herbs.** Select high-grade and, where possible, organic herbs to ensure they are free from pesticides and other harmful substances.

4. **Experiment with blends.** Get creative and experiment with blending different botanicals together to create unique flavor profiles and enhance the synergistic effects of the ingredients. Always refer to our blending guide in Chapter 1 or seek professional advice.

5. **Incorporate adaptogenic herbs.** Incorporate adaptogens like the ones we listed in our mushroom tea recipe. Adaptogens can help your body adapt to stress and promote a sense of calm and balance, both of which are beneficial to overall brain health.

6. **Be consistent.** When it comes to reaping the benefits of herbal teas for brain health, consistency is key. Drink herbal tea regularly to maximize its potential benefits.

Remember to consult with a healthcare professional or herbalist if you have any specific health concerns or if you are taking medications that may interact with botanicals.

WRAPPING UP CHAPTER 11

We've hit a total of 70 recipes, plus double that number and more if you mix and match the ingredients according to your own taste and needs. We would love to know what you think of our recipe selection, so when you leave a review, be sure to mention it.

Up next, we have our bonus chapter!

CHAPTER 11 GLOSSARY

Ashwagandha: Reduces oxidative stress associated with Alzheimer's disease.

Bacopa Monnieri: Contains anti-inflammatory and cognition-enhancing properties.

Chaga Mushroom: Antioxidant-rich, supports brain health.

Cinnamon: Improves brain health, reduces oxidative stress, and possibly prevents dementia.

Ginger: Reduces oxidative stress and protects against neurode-generative diseases.

Ginkgo Biloba: Stimulates circulation and promotes blood flow to the brain.

Ginseng: May prevent memory loss and reduce age-related memory decline.

Gotu Kola: Inhibits Alzheimer's-associated oxidative stress and improves cognitive function.

Green Tea: Contains antioxidants that reduce oxidative damage and inflammation in the brain.

Lemon Balm: May improve cognitive function and relieve symptoms of mild depression and anxiety.

Lion's Mane Mushroom: Enhances memory, focus, cognition, and neurogenesis.

Nutmeg: Contains myristicin, which helps prevent the formation of beta-amyloid plaques.

Peppermint: Enhances cognitive function and boosts recall.

Reishi Mushroom: Supports immune function, circulation, and mood elevation.

Rosemary: Contains the neuroprotective compound carnosic acid, which protects the brain from free radical damage.

Saffron: Supports brain aging, focus, and mood and aids in memory support.

Sage: May improve cognition and aid in the treatment of Alzheimer's disease.

Turmeric: Contains curcumin, which improves brain health and clears beta-amyloid plaques.

BONUS CHAPTER

W hen something is really good, we don't want it to end. It's like enjoying that second cup of tea, reading one more page, or looking for one more recipe. With that in mind, we have our Bonus Chapter. Here's what you can look forward to:

- ✔ Recommendations for safe sites to purchase herbs
- ✔ Refined sugar alternatives for those who prefer sweeter teas
- ✔ Turning herbal teas into smoothies—including 10 unique smoothie recipes!
- ✔ 5 More herbal tea recipes
- ✔ Gadgets for herbal tea lovers

RECOMMENDED SITES FOR BUYING HERBS AND TEAS

If you can, grow some herbs in your garden, in window boxes in your kitchen, or on your patio. There's nothing quite as lovely as snipping some fresh lavender, peppermint, or rosemary and using it to make a cup of herbal tea.

If you want to know more about growing your own herbs, especially for medicinal purposes, look up our other book, *Grow Your Own Herbal Medicine: Easily Create Your Own Sustainable Herb Garden to Support Health, Treat Common Ailments and Become Self-Sufficient.*

If you are unable to grow your own herbs, then be sure to buy your herbs or teas from reputable suppliers. As we mentioned earlier in the book, the quality of the ingredients you use is crucial to achieving maximum health benefits.

Using high-quality herbs in herbal teas is crucial not only for the effectiveness of the tea but also for your safety. Low-quality herbs and teas may contain harmful contaminants, such as heavy metals and pesticides, which can be detrimental to your health in the long term. Therefore, it's essential to purchase herbs and teas from reputable sources that guarantee the purity and quality of their products.

The following are not the only trustworthy suppliers out there, but they are the ones that come recommended by our readers:

- Mountain Rose Herbs
- Iherb.com
- Elk Mountain Herbs
- Frontier Co-op

REFINED SUGAR ALTERNATIVES

Adding refined sugar to herbal tea can diminish the potential health benefits of the medicinal herbs. Herbal teas are most often consumed for their therapeutic properties, and including high-quality ingredients is essential for maximizing their positive effects. Adding refined sugar can counteract the goodness of the herbs and may contribute to negative health effects associated with excessive sugar consumption.

Refined sugar is known to be high in calories and devoid of nutritional value. Consuming excess sugar can lead to weight gain, inflammation, and an increased risk of chronic diseases like diabetes and heart disease. Furthermore, sugar can cause energy crashes and disrupt focus and concentration, which may be counterproductive to the intended benefits of herbal teas.

If you prefer a sweeter taste, consider using natural sweeteners that can provide a touch of sweetness without the negative effects associated with refined sugar. However, be mindful of the overall sugar intake and consume herbal teas in moderation as part of a balanced diet.

Let's take a closer look at some refined sugar alternatives:

Stevia

Stevia is a natural sweetener derived from the leaves of the South American shrub *Stevia rebaudiana*. It is calorie-free and significantly sweeter than sugar. Stevia has been shown to help prevent weight gain and reduce blood sugar levels (Kubala, 2023).

Sugar alcohols

Sugar alcohols, such as erythritol and xylitol, are naturally found in fruits and vegetables. They have fewer calories than sugar and don't significantly affect blood sugar levels. Sugar alcohols are also tooth-friendly and are often used by those with diabetes (Kubala, 2023).

Maple syrup

Maple syrup is a natural sweetener made from the sap of maple trees. It contains some beneficial compounds like antioxidants and minerals. Although it still contains sugar, using small amounts of maple syrup can provide a natural sweetness with added nutrients (Kubala, 2023)

Honey

Honey is a sweet and flavorful alternative to refined sugar. It contains antioxidants and has potential antibacterial properties.

However, it is important to note that honey is still high in sugar and should be consumed in moderation (Team, 2023).

Choose unpasteurized honey.

The natural properties and nutritional content of unpasteurized honey make it a preferred choice for those seeking the potential health benefits associated with honey consumption. In the context of honey, pasteurization involves heating the honey to a specific temperature for a certain duration to eliminate any potential pathogens and extend its shelf life. The process may also involve filtration to remove impurities such as pollen and wax particles.

Unpasteurized or raw honey is minimally processed and comes straight from the hive. It contains a wide range of nutrients, including amino acids, minerals, vitamins, enzymes, and antioxidants. The natural processing of raw honey preserves these beneficial compounds.

Raw honey contains various bioactive plant compounds, including polyphenols, which act as antioxidants. These antioxidants have been associated with reduced inflammation and a lower risk of heart disease and certain types of cancer (Berry, 2019).

Raw honey maintains its natural properties, including bee pollen and propolis, which have additional health benefits. Bee pollen has antioxidant and anti-inflammatory properties, while propolis has antimicrobial properties (Berry, 2019).

Raw honey tends to have more variation in color and texture, as it reflects the specific flowers the bees have pollinated. It has a more robust and complex flavor profile compared to pasteurized honey, which is often processed to have a consistent appearance and texture (Berry, 2019).

Chose local honey.

Have you heard of immunotherapy? It involves ingesting small amounts of an allergen to gradually develop tolerance. Using locally sourced honey to sweeten your tea is a kind of immunotherapy because the honey contains traces of the pollen you may be allergic to. Plus, it reduces your carbon footprint while supporting the local beekeeper.

Don't boil honey.

Adding honey to boiling hot tea may lead to the degradation of heat-sensitive components in the honey, potentially diminishing its nutritional and therapeutic properties. To preserve the honey's properties, let your tea cool for a bit before adding the honey. However, be aware that honey possesses natural antimicrobial properties, which, when added to liquids become enhanced, potentially providing benefits in terms of soothing a sore throat or alleviating cough symptoms.

Coconut sugar

Coconut sugar is derived from the sap of coconut palm trees. It contains small amounts of nutrients like iron, zinc, and potassium. Coconut sugar has a lower glycemic index compared to refined sugar, meaning it causes a slower rise in blood sugar levels.

Monk fruit extract

Monk fruit extract is a natural sweetener derived from the monk fruit. It is calorie-free and has been used for centuries in traditional Chinese medicine. Monk fruit extract provides sweetness without impacting blood sugar levels.

Dates

Dates are a natural sweetener with a rich caramel-like flavor. They are packed with fiber, vitamins, and minerals, making them a healthier choice compared to refined sugar. They can't necessarily be used to sweeten your herbal teas, but they can be used in baking or blended into smoothies.

When incorporating these alternatives into your diet, it's important to remember that while they may offer some potential health benefits, any type of sweetener should still be consumed in moderation. It's always a good idea to consult with a healthcare professional or registered dietitian to determine the most suitable options for your specific dietary needs and health goals.

TURNING HERBAL TEAS INTO SMOOTHIES

Another way to incorporate herbal teas into your diet is to turn them into smoothies. Tea smoothies are not only delicious but also full of nature's goodness, making them an excellent choice for breakfast or a nutrient-packed treat any other time.

Tea smoothies offer all the health benefits we've already covered, plus the added nutrients found in fruit! The best part —tea smoothies are incredibly versatile. You can customize them with your favorite fruits, vegetables, and even add-ons like extracts, cocoa powder, or spices.

If you want to incorporate protein, add milk, yogurt, nuts, or protein powder. To enhance sweetness, use naturally sweet fruits or one of the sugar alternatives we covered earlier.

Adjust the texture by adding ice and liquids for a slushy consistency or skip the extra liquids for a thick and creamy smoothie. Get creative and enjoy the endless possibilities of tea smoothies.

Let's take a look at some smoothie ideas using some of our herbal tea recipes:

71. Digestive Health Smoothie

Your ingredients:

- Digestive Harmony Tea (Tea 6)
- 1 cup mixed berries
- 1 banana
- ½ cucumber

The best way to make it:

1. Make the Digestive Harmony Tea as directed and allow it to cool or add ice.
2. In a blender, combine the mixed berries, banana, cucumber, and tea.
3. Blend on high until smooth and creamy.
4. Pour and enjoy!

You can mix and match any of the following additional ingredients for digestive health: pineapple, papaya, spinach, or kale.

72. Flower-Filled Calming Smoothie

Your ingredients:

- Flower Filled Calming Tea (Tea 8)
- 2 citrus fruits, peeled
- 1 tsp cocoa powder

The best way to make it:

1. Make the Flower-Filled Calming Tea as directed and allow it to cool or add ice.
2. In a blender, combine the peeled citrus fruit, cocoa powder, and tea.
3. Blend on high until smooth and creamy.
4. Pour and enjoy!

You can mix and match the following additional ingredients for a calming smoothie: avocado, berries, pumpkin seeds, spinach, or kale.

73. Bittersweet Relaxing Smoothie

Your ingredients:

- Calm and Sleepy Tea (Tea 18)
- 2 tablespoons pure aloe vera gel
- 1 ripe avocado

The best way to make it:

1. Make the relaxing tea as directed and allow it to cool or add ice.
2. In a blender, combine the aloe vera, avocado, and tea.
3. Blend on high until smooth and creamy.
4. Pour and enjoy!

You can mix and match the following additional ingredients for a relaxing smoothie: cauliflower, spinach, pumpkin, mango, carrots, or cucumber.

74. Hormone-Balancing Smoothie

Your ingredients:

- Hormone-Balancing Blend (Tea 26)
- 1 cup blueberries
- 1 cup cauliflower

The best way to make it:

1. Make the hormone balancing tea as directed and allow it to cool or add ice.
2. In a blender, combine the blueberries, cauliflower, and tea.
3. Blend on high until smooth and creamy.
4. Pour and enjoy!

You can mix and match the following additional ingredients for a hormone balancing smoothie: flaxseed, chia seeds, or spinach.

75. Skin and Hair Health Smoothie

Your ingredients:

- Nourishing Beau-Tea (Tea 35)
- 1 carrot, diced
- ½ a pineapple, cut into chunks

The best way to make it:

1. Make the skin and hair health tea as directed and allow it to cool or add ice.
2. In a blender, combine the carrot, pineapple, and tea.
3. Blend on high until smooth and creamy.
4. Pour and enjoy!

You can mix and match the following additional ingredients for a skin and hair health smoothie: berries, spinach, avocado, or cucumber.

76. Pain and Inflammation Relief Smoothie

Your ingredients:

- Pain Relief Tea (Tea 36)
- 1 cup berries
- ½ a pineapple, cut into chunks

The best way to make it:

1. Make the pain and inflammation tea as directed and allow it to cool or add ice.
2. In a blender, combine the berries, pineapple, and tea.
3. Blend on high until smooth and creamy.
4. Pour and enjoy!

You can mix and match the following additional ingredients for a pain and inflammation relief smoothie: spinach or avocado.

77. Green Energy Boosting Smoothie

Your ingredients:

- 1 cup matcha green tea
- 2 cups kale
- 1 cup mixed berries

The best way to make it:

1. Make the matcha tea as directed and allow to cool or add ice.
2. In a blender, combine the kale, mixed berries, and matcha tea.
3. Blend on high until smooth and creamy.
4. Pour and enjoy!

You can mix and match the following additional ingredients for an energy and focus boosting smoothie: banana, spinach, pineapple, oranges, mango, or avocado.

78. Decongestant Smoothie

Your ingredients:

- Combat Congestion Tea (Tea 50)
- 1 citrus fruit
- 1 apple
- 1 carrot, diced

The best way to make it:

1. Make the decongestant tea as directed and allow to cool or add ice.
2. In a blender, combine the peeled citrus fruit, apple, carrot, and tea.
3. Blend on high until smooth and creamy.
4. Pour and enjoy!

You can mix and match the following additional ingredients for an anti-allergy smoothie: pineapple, berries, spinach, and kale.

79. Athletic Performance Smoothie

Your ingredients:

- Power Boost Tea (Tea 58)
- 2 tablespoons of nut butter
- 1 banana

The best way to make it:

1. Make the athletic performance tea as directed and allow to cool or add ice.
2. In a blender, combine the nut butter, banana, and tea.
3. Blend on high until smooth and creamy.
4. Pour and enjoy!

You can mix and match the following additional ingredients for a performance enhancing smoothie: protein rich ingredients like Greek yoghurt, whey powder or plant-based protein powder, berries, spinach, kale, oranges, or chia seeds.

80. Brain Health Smoothie

Your ingredients:

- Memory Protect Tea (Tea 68)
- 2 cups spinach
- walnuts

The best way to make it:

1. Make the brain health tea as directed and allow to cool or add ice.
2. In a blender, combine the spinach, walnuts, and tea.
3. Blend on high until smooth and creamy.
4. Pour and enjoy!

You can mix and match the following additional ingredients for a performance enhancing smoothie: kale, berries, almond butter, or matcha powder.

MORE HERBAL TEA RECIPES

While we're in the recipe flow, to follow is a selection of herbal tea recipes that don't quite fit in any of our previous chapter categories:

81. Tea to Combat Vertigo

Your ingredients:

- 1–2 tsp *Ginkgo biloba*, and/or
- 1–2 tsp butcher's broom, and/or
- 1-inch fresh ginger root, sliced
- 2 cups water

The best way to make it:

1. In a pot, bring water to a boil.
2. Add the ginkgo, butcher's broom, or ginger to the pot.
3. Let steep for 5–10 minutes.
4. Strain and serve.

A snippet of insight into the ingredients:

As we have already discovered, *Ginkgo biloba* is known to improve blood flow to the brain and can, therefore, alleviate dizziness.

Ginger root has been used in Asian traditional medicine to treat dizziness, including vertigo, because it improves blood circulation in the inner ear and brain.

Butcher's broom is another herb that can be used as an herbal remedy for vertigo. It helps alleviate disorders in the brain and inner ear by acting as a vasodilator (Team, 2020).

82. Tea to Alleviate Constipation

Your ingredients:

- 1–2 tsp peppermint leaf
- 1–2 tsp dandelion root
- 1-inch fresh ginger root, sliced
- 2 cups water

The best way to make it:

1. In a pot, bring water to a boil.
2. Add the peppermint, dandelion, and ginger to the pot.
3. Let steep for 10 minutes.
4. Strain and serve.

A snippet of insight into the ingredients:

We learned previously that peppermint tea has soothing properties and can help relieve digestive issues, including constipation. It may help relax the muscles of the gastrointestinal tract, promoting smoother bowel movements.

Dandelion root tea is believed to have a mild laxative effect and can help stimulate digestion (Roland, 2019). Just be aware that dandelion has diuretic properties, and dehydration may exacerbate constipation.

Ginger has been traditionally used to aid digestion and relieve constipation. We have previously read about its anti-inflammatory properties; these may help promote regular bowel movements and reduce bloating.

Other herbal teas that can relieve constipation include senna, cascara sagrada, and licorice root.

83. Tea for Headache Relief

Your ingredients:

- 1–2 tsp willow bark
- 1–2 tsp peppermint
- 2 cups water

The best way to make it:

1. In a pot, bring water to a boil.
2. Add the willow bark and peppermint.
3. Let steep for 5–10 minutes.
4. Strain and serve.

A snippet of insight into the ingredients:

Willow bark contains salicin, which is similar to the active ingredient in aspirin. Willow bark tea may have pain-relieving properties and can potentially help alleviate headaches (Moore, 2020). However, it's important to exercise caution when using willow bark, as it may interact with certain medications and should be avoided by individuals with certain medical conditions.

Peppermint oil applied topically to the forehead has been shown to ease tension headaches, and there is some evidence suggesting that peppermint tea may have pain-relieving effects (Osborn, 2019). It's worth noting that peppermint tea, which is generally safe for consumption, is different from medicinal peppermint oil, which is typically stronger. When using peppermint oil, a carrier oil is highly recommended because of the oil's potency.

Other herbal teas that may alleviate headaches include ginger, chamomile, butterbur, and feverfew.

84. Tea for Oral Health

Your ingredients:

- 1–2 tsp dried peppermint leaf or 3–5 fresh peppermint leaves
- 1 bag green tea
- 2 cups water

The best way to make it:

1. In a pot, bring water to a boil.
2. Add the peppermint and green tea.
3. Let steep for 5 minutes.
4. Strain and serve.

A snippet of insight into the ingredients:

Peppermint tea contains menthol and other beneficial compounds, and green tea may promote oral health by reducing the risk of gum disease and improving dental health (Ruggeri, 2023).

Other teas that can aid in oral health include ginger, chamomile, hibiscus, and sage.

85. Tea for Eye Health

Your ingredients:

- 1–2 tsp eyebright
- 1 tsp *Ginkgo biloba*
- 2 cups water

The best way to make it:

1. In a pot, bring water to a boil.
2. Add the eyebright and ginkgo.
3. Let steep for 5–10 minutes.
4. Strain and serve.

A snippet of insight into the ingredients:

The name says it all—eyebright is an herb with a long history of medicinal use for eye ailments, particularly conjunctivitis (redness and discharge caused by eye irritation).

Apart from all the other benefits we have come to know it possesses, ginkgo may improve blood flow to the retina, and it has been studied for its potential benefits in supporting eye health. Preliminary research suggests that *Ginkgo biloba* extracts may improve vision in people with glaucoma. It also has antioxidant properties and can protect nerve cells, including those in the eye (White, n.d.).

Other teas that are good for eye health include blueberry, wolfberry, and green tea.

TEATIME GADGETS

Whether you are a tea drinker or you're looking for a cool gift idea for a tea-drinking loved one, here are some teatime gadgets to stir your imagination:

Electric kettle

An electric kettle is a convenient and efficient gadget for heating water to the perfect temperature for brewing tea. Look for kettles with temperature control options to ensure optimal brewing for different types of tea.

Tea infuser or steeper

A tea infuser or steeper is a handy gadget for brewing loose-leaf tea. It allows the tea leaves to steep and release their flavors while keeping them contained. There are various designs available, such as stainless-steel infusers or teapots with built-in infusers.

Reusable tea bags

Unlike traditional tea bags that are single-use and disposable, reusable tea bags are designed to be washed and reused, making them a more sustainable option. Reusable tea bags are typically made of materials like cotton or other fabric, and they often have a drawstring or closure mechanism to keep the tea leaves contained during brewing.

Bamboo tea tumbler

A bamboo tumbler is a great option for tea lovers who enjoy taking their tea on the go. These tumblers often have built-in filters or infusers, allowing you to brew tea directly in the tumbler and enjoy it throughout the day.

Tea advent calendar

A tea advent calendar makes a delightful gift, especially during the holiday season. It offers a selection of teas for each day leading up to Christmas, allowing tea lovers to explore and enjoy a variety of flavors.

Tea set

A tea set, complete with a teapot and matching cups, is a thoughtful gift for tea enthusiasts. Look for elegant and beautifully designed teapot sets that add a touch of charm to teatime.

Tea subscription box

A tea subscription box is a gift that keeps on giving. It allows tea lovers to discover new flavors and varieties of tea regularly. Subscription boxes often include curated selections of teas based on personal preferences and tasting profiles.

Tea accessories

Consider other tea accessories like teaspoons, honey spoons, and matcha bowl sets. These items can add fun and convenience to the tea-drinking experience.

WRAPPING UP OUR BONUS CHAPTER

Well, that was a full chapter! It covered where to shop for high-quality herbs, healthy refined sugar alternatives, how to turn tea into smoothies (including 10 mouth-watering recipes), another 5 herbal tea recipes, and gadgets for tea lovers.

BONUS CHAPTER GLOSSARY

Butcher's Broom: Acts as a vasodilator, supports blood circulation, and can help alleviate disorders in the brain and inner ear related to vertigo.

Dandelion Root: Supports liver function, stimulates digestion, and may have a mild laxative effect, helping alleviate constipation.

Eyebright: Traditionally used for eye health, it may help alleviate eye strain, redness, and irritation.

Ginger Root: Improves blood circulation, aids digestion, reduces inflammation, and may help alleviate dizziness or vertigo.

Ginkgo Biloba: Improves blood flow to the brain, enhances cognitive function, and may alleviate dizziness or vertigo.

Peppermint Leaf: Soothes the digestive system, aids digestion and may help alleviate constipation or digestive discomfort.

Turmeric: Contains curcumin, which has anti-inflammatory and antioxidant properties, supports digestion, and promotes overall health.

Valerian: Has calming and soothing effects on the nervous system, helps reduce anxiety, and promotes better sleep.

Willow Bark: Contains salicin, which has pain-relieving properties similar to aspirin and may help alleviate headaches and reduce pain and inflammation.

Yerba Mate: Contains caffeine and other stimulating compounds that provide energy and focus, improve mental clarity, and support weight management.

PAYING IT FORWARD

I have an important question for you! If you could take a moment and help someone empower their life, heal their mind and body and it only took a few moments of your time, would you consider it?

That is exactly what you would be doing by leaving a review of this book on Amazon. If you are enjoying this information and finding the resources helpful, please take a moment to share your experience by posting a review on Amazon via the link or QR code below.

As a self-published author, I rely solely on you, my kind and caring readers to help me spread the word. Your willingness to review will assist others on their journey to become more self-sufficient, confident, and empowered by using and growing these powerfully healing plants! Many thanks to you!

https://geni.us/AmazonReviewLinkLove

CONCLUSION

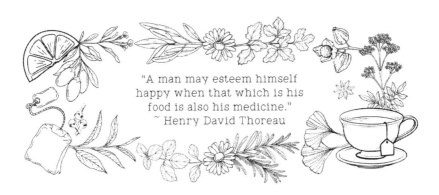

"A man may esteem himself
happy when that which is his
food is also his medicine."
~ Henry David Thoreau

We have completed our journey into the wonderful world of
herbal teas. Throughout this book, we explored the incredible
benefits that these herbal preparations offer for our overall
health and well-being. From soothing digestion and promoting
detoxification to boosting immunity and relieving stress, herbal
teas have proven to be nature's gift for nurturing our bodies
and minds.

In Chapter 1, we laid the foundation by introducing the basic principles of herbal teas. We discussed the importance of understanding different types of herbs, choosing the right ones for our needs, and blending them safely. We also provided cautionary information to ensure you approach herbal teas with knowledge and care. Armed with this understanding, you are ready to embark on a lifelong journey of tea exploration.

In the subsequent chapters, we provided recipes and delved into some diverse categories of herbal teas. We discovered how they can support our digestion, aid in detoxification, provide relief from pain and inflammation, boost our immunity, and offer solace during times of stress and restlessness. We explored the nurturing properties of herbal teas for women's health, their ability to enhance our skin and hair care routines, and their contribution to improve sleep and relaxation. We also explored their potential to increase energy and focus, alleviate seasonal allergies, enhance athletic performance, and support brain health. Each chapter offered a collection of recipes that showcased the versatility of herbal teas.

But our journey didn't end there; as a special treat, we prepared a bonus chapter to enrich your herbal tea experience. There, you found lots of additional information, more delightful tea recipes, and some exciting recipes for herbal tea smoothies. Let your taste buds and creativity run wild as you indulge in these health-giving concoctions.

As we conclude, we want to emphasize the incredible benefits that incorporating herbal teas into your daily life can bring.

These brews have the power to uplift your spirits, calm your mind, rejuvenate your body, and awaken your senses. The magic lies in their natural compounds, carefully nurtured by Mother Nature herself, working in harmony with your body's needs.

We encourage you to embrace herbal teas as an integral part of your daily routine. Let them be your companions during quiet moments of reflection, shared conversations with loved ones, or simply as a comforting pause in a busy day. Sip mindfully, allowing the warmth to permeate your being, and savor the essence of each cup.

Remember, the path to a healthier you is built upon the choices you make every day. By incorporating herbal teas into your lifestyle, you are nurturing yourself. Your body and mind will thank you as you experience the transformative power of these gentle yet potent brews.

If you want to learn more about the wonder of herbs, read our book, *Herbalism for Beginners: Discover Hundreds of Secret Herbal Remedies and Medicinal Plants to Heal Naturally, Create Self-sufficiency and Easily Build Your At-home Apothecary in as Little as 7 Days*

Also, get in touch with us by joining our Facebook group: *Herbalism and Natural Living for Beginners*. We look forward to meeting you there, reading your herbal insights, and sharing our herbal news.

If this book inspired you, helped you or made you feel more confident in your healing herbal journey, please scan the QR code below and leave a review on Amazon so that other people in need of natural remedies for various health issues can take the necessary steps toward a healthier, herbal lifestyle.

May your teacup always overflow with serenity, vitality, and the wonders of herbal teas!

REFERENCES

Abubakar, S. M., Ukeyima, M. T., Spencer, J. P. E., & Lovegrove, J. A. (2019, February 5). Acute effects of Hibiscus Sabdariffa Calyces on postprandial blood pressure, vascular function, blood lipids, biomarkers of insulin resistance and inflammation in humans. Nutrients. https://www.ncbi.nlm.nih.gov/pmc/articles/PMC6412462/

Ajmera, R. (2020, February 25). 7 proven health benefits of Matcha Tea. Healthline. https://www.healthline.com/nutrition/7-benefits-of-matcha-tea

Ajmera, R. (2023, March 15). The 10 best foods to eat if you have arthritis. Healthline. https://www.healthline.com/health/foods-for-arthritis

Alammar, N., Wang, L., Saberi, B., Nanavati, J., Holtmann, G., Shinohara, R. T., & Mullin, G. E. (2019, January 17). The impact of peppermint oil on irritable bowel syndrome: A meta-analysis of the pooled clinical data. BMC complementary and alternative medicine. https://www.ncbi.nlm.nih.gov/pmc/articles/PMC6337770/

Ali, B. H., Blunden, G., Tanira, M. O., & Nemmar, A. (2008). Some phytochemical, pharmacological and toxicological properties of ginger (Zingiber officinale Roscoe): A review of recent research. Food and Chemical Toxicology, 46(2), 409-420.

Babu, P. V. A., & Liu, D. (2008). Green tea catechins and cardiovascular health: An update. Current medicinal chemistry https://www.ncbi.nlm.nih.gov/pmc/articles/PMC2748751/

Berry, J. (2019, April 15). Raw Honey vs. regular honey: Benefits, risks, and uses. Medical News Today. https://www.medicalnewstoday.com/articles/324966

Chandrasekhar, K., Kapoor, J., & Anishetty, S. (2012, July). A prospective, randomized double-blind, placebo-controlled study. https://pubmed.ncbi.nlm.nih.gov/23439798/

Chumpitazi, B. P., Kearns, G. L., & Shulman, R. J. (2018, March). Review article: The physiological effects and safety of peppermint oil and its efficacy in irritable bowel syndrome and other functional disorders. Alimentary pharmacology & therapeutics. https://www.ncbi.nlm.nih.gov/pmc/arti cles/PMC5814329/

Cohen, M. M. (2014). Tulsi - Ocimum sanctum: A herb for all reasons. Journal of Ayurveda and integrative medicine. https://www.ncbi.nlm.nih.gov/ pmc/articles/PMC4296439/

Complete Beginners Guide to Herbalism: 171 Herbal Remedies & Medicinal Plants to Heal Naturally, Create Self-Sufficiency & Build Your At-Home Apothecary Even if You Have No Experience. 2023, January 31. My Book

Cronkleton, E. (2019, March 8). Lemon Balm: Uses, benefits, and more. Healthline. https://www.healthline.com/health/lemon-balm-uses

da Silva, W., Machado, Á. S., & Souza, M. A. (2018). Effect of green tea extract supplementation on exercise-induced delayed onset muscle soreness and muscular damage. Physiology & behavior. https://pubmed.ncbi.nlm.nih. gov/29746891/

Davidson, K. (2019, December 4). Rose hips: Benefits, forms, uses, and side effects. Healthline. https://www.healthline.com/nutrition/rose-hips

Elay, E. (2011, June). Food & Function Blog. Publishing Blogs. https://blogs. rsc.org/fo/2011/06/23/chaga-mushrooms-could-aid-memory-loss-and-other-cognitive-functions/?doing_wp_cron=1685973948. 2632589340209960937500

Elliott, B. (2023, March 20). 5 ways Chamomile Tea Benefits Your Health. Healthline. https://www.healthline.com/nutrition/5-benefits-of-chamomile-tea

Forbes. (2023, February 6). Cinnamon improves your memory and cognition. Forbes. https://www.forbes.com/sites/grrlscientist/2023/02/04/cinna mon-improves-your-memory-and-cognition/?sh=4c6b44b821ec

Ghasemzadeh Rahbardar, M., & Hosseinzadeh, H. (2020, September). Therapeutic effects of rosemary (rosmarinus officinalis L.) and its active constituents on nervous system disorders. Iranian journal of basic medical sciences. https://www.ncbi.nlm.nih.gov/pmc/articles/PMC7491497/

Goodson, A. (2018, July 4). Why turmeric and black pepper is a powerful combination. Healthline. https://www.healthline.com/nutrition/turmeric-and-black-pepper

Got allergies? here are the best herbs to alleviate them. Boochcraft. (2020, April 17). https://boochcraft.com/blog/handy-tips/got-allergies-here-are-the-best-herbs-to-alleviate-them/

Gray, P. (2004). Herbal Fallacies. CRC Press.

Gxaba, N., & Manganyi, M. C. (2022, June 6). The fight against infection and pain: Devil's Claw (harpagophytum procumbens) a rich source of anti-inflammatory activity: 2011-2022. Molecules (Basel, Switzerland). https://www.ncbi.nlm.nih.gov/pmc/articles/PMC9182060/

Health Library. (n.d.). Lemon Balm. Mount Sinai Health System. https://www.mountsinai.org/health-library/herb/lemon-balm

Heitz, D. (2019a, April 1). Can Dong Quai help with menopause? Healthline. https://www.healthline.com/health/dong-quai-ancient-mystery

Jackson, P. A., Forster, J., Khan, J., Pouchieu, C., Dubreuil, S., Gaudout, D., Moras, B., Pourtau, L., Joffre, F., Vaysse, C., Bertrand, K., Abrous, H., Vauzour, D., Brossaud, J., Corcuff, J. B., Capuron, L., & Kennedy, D. O. (2021, February 1). Effects of saffron extract supplementation on mood, well-being, and response to a psychosocial stressor in healthy adults: A randomized, double-blind, Parallel Group, clinical trial. Frontiers in nutrition. https://www.ncbi.nlm.nih.gov/pmc/articles/PMC7882499/

Jacob, L. (2023b, May 18). The best herbal teas for gym goers. NutraTea. https://nutratea.co.uk/herbal-teas-for-gym-goers/

Jalalyazdi, M., Ramezani, J., Izadi-Moud, A., Madani-Sani, F., Shahlaei, S., & Ghiasi, S. S. (2019). Effect of hibiscus SABDARIFFA on blood pressure in patients with stage 1 hypertension. Journal of advanced pharmaceutical technology & research. https://www.ncbi.nlm.nih.gov/pmc/articles/PMC6621350/

Jamshidi, N., & Cohen, M. M. (2017). The clinical efficacy and safety of tulsi in humans: A systematic review of the literature. Evidence-based complementary and alternative medicine : eCAM. https://www.ncbi.nlm.nih.gov/pmc/articles/PMC5376420/

Janda, K., Wojtkowska, K., Jakubczyk, K., Antoniewicz, J., & Skonieczna-Żydecka, K. (2020, December 19). passiflora incarnata in neuropsychiatric disorders-A systematic review. Nutrients. https://www.ncbi.nlm.nih.gov/pmc/articles/PMC7766837/

Joubert, E., Gelderblom, W., Louw, A., & de Beer, D. (2008, October). South African herbal teas: Aspalathus linearis, Cyclopia spp. and Athrixia phylicoides--a review. Journal of ethnopharmacology. https://pubmed.ncbi.nlm.nih.gov/18621121/

Kanadys, W., Barańska, A., Błaszczuk, A., Polz-Dacewicz, M., Drop, B., Kanecki, K., & Malm, M. (2021, April 11). Evaluation of clinical meaningfulness of Red Clover (trifolium pratense L.) extract to relieve hot flushes and menopausal symptoms in peri- and post-menopausal women: A systematic review and meta-analysis of randomized controlled trials. Nutrients. https://www.ncbi.nlm.nih.gov/pmc/articles/PMC8069620/

Kawatra, P., & Rajagopalan, R. (2015, June). Cinnamon: Mystic powers of a minute ingredient. Pharmacognosy research. https://www.ncbi.nlm.nih.gov/pmc/articles/PMC4466762/

Kidd, P. M. (2005, December). Neurodegeneration from mitochondrial insufficiency: Nutrients, stem cells, growth factors, and prospects for brain rebuilding using Integrative Management. Alternative medicine review: a journal of clinical therapeutic. https://pubmed.ncbi.nlm.nih.gov/16366737/

Kluger, J. (1997, May 12). Dr. Andrew Weil: Mr. natural. Time. https://content.time.com/time/subscriber/article/0,33009,986319-2,00.html

Koulivand, P. H., Khaleghi Ghadiri, M., & Gorji, A. (2013). Lavender and the nervous system. Evidence-based complementary and alternative medicine: eCAM. https://www.ncbi.nlm.nih.gov/pmc/articles/PMC3612440/

Kubala, J. (2020, October 5). The 10 best herbs to boost energy and focus. Healthline. https://www.healthline.com/nutrition/herbs-for-energy#2.-Sage

Kubala, J. (2022, January 6). 4 benefits of maca root (and potential side effects). Healthline. https://www.healthline.com/nutrition/benefits-of-maca-root

Kubala, J. (2022, January 7). 9 proven health benefits of ashwagandha. Healthline. https://www.healthline.com/nutrition/ashwagandha

Kubala, J. (2023, April 19). 10 alternatives to refined sugar. Healthline. https://www.healthline.com/nutrition/natural-sugar-substitutes

Langade, D., Kanchi, S., Salve, J., Debnath, K., & Ambegaokar, D. (2019, September 28). Efficacy and safety of ashwagandha (Withania somnifera) root extract in insomnia and anxiety: A double-blind, randomized, placebo-controlled study. Cureus. https://www.ncbi.nlm.nih.gov/pmc/articles/PMC6827862/

Liu, L., Liu, C., Wang, Y., Wang, P., Li, Y., & Li, B. (2015, July). Herbal Medicine for anxiety, depression and insomnia. Current neuropharmacology. https://www.ncbi.nlm.nih.gov/pmc/articles/PMC4790408/

Liu, Y., Wang, J., Wang, W., Zhang, H., Zhang, X., & Han, C. (2015). The chemical constituents and pharmacological actions of cordyceps sinensis. Evidence-based complementary and alternative medicine: eCAM. https://www.ncbi.nlm.nih.gov/pmc/articles/PMC4415478/

Maeda-Yamamoto, M. (2013). The benefits of green tea catechins on the symptoms of the common cold and influenza. Journal of Functional Foods, 5(2), 789-798.

Marshall, A. C. (2020, March 2). Traditional Chinese Medicine and Clinical Pharmacology. Drug Discovery and Evaluation: Methods in Clinical Pharmacology. https://www.ncbi.nlm.nih.gov/pmc/articles/PMC7356495/

Mashhadi, N. S., Ghiasvand, R., Askari, G., Hariri, M., Darvishi, L., & Mofid, M. R. (2013, April). Anti-oxidative and anti-inflammatory effects of ginger in health and physical activity: Review of current evidence. International journal of preventive medicine. https://www.ncbi.nlm.nih.gov/pmc/articles/PMC3665023/

McKay, D. L., & Blumberg, J. B. (2006). A review of the bioactivity and potential health benefits of peppermint tea (Mentha piperita L.). Phytotherapy Research, 20(8), 619-633.

Mehta, F. (2021, January 20). What you should know about the benefits and risks of L-Theanine. Healthline. https://www.healthline.com/health/l-theanine

Meissner, H. O., Mrozikiewicz, P., Bobkiewicz-Kozlowska, T., Mscisz, A., Kedzia, B., Lowicka, A., Reich-Bilinska, H., Kapczynski, W., & Barchia, I. (2006a, September). Hormone-balancing effect of pre-gelatinized organic maca (Lepidium Peruvianum Chacon): (I) biochemical and pharmacodynamic study on maca using clinical laboratory model on ovariectomized rats. International journal of biomedical science: IJBS. https://www.ncbi.nlm.nih.gov/pmc/articles/PMC3614604/

Michalak, M. (2022, January 6). Plant-derived antioxidants: Significance in skin health and the ageing process. International journal of molecular sciences. https://www.ncbi.nlm.nih.gov/pmc/articles/PMC8776015/

Mirmosayyeb, O., Tanhaei, A., Sohrabi, H. R., Martins, R. N., Tanhaei, M., Najafi, M. A., Safaei, A., & Meamar, R. (2017, February 7). Possible role of common spices as a preventive and therapeutic agent for alzheimer's disease. International journal of preventive medicine. https://www.ncbi.nlm.nih.gov/pmc/articles/PMC5320868/

Mishra, S., & Palanivelu, K. (2008, January). The effect of curcumin (turmeric) on alzheimer's disease: An overview. Annals of Indian Academy of Neurology. https://www.ncbi.nlm.nih.gov/pmc/articles/PMC2781139/

Mona, B. (2021, February 26). 11 best teas to kick those allergies this spring.

Greatist.   https://greatist.com/health/tea-for-allergies#best-tea-for-allergies

Moore, A. (2020, October 20). 6 expert-approved teas to soothe headaches once (or before) they hit. mindbodygreen. https://www.mindbodygreen.com/articles/tea-for-headaches

Mori K, Inatomi S, Ouchi K et al. (2009) Improving effects of the mushroom Yamabushitake (Hericium erinaceus) on mild cognitive impairment: a double-blind placebo-controlled clinical trial. Phytother Res 23, 367-372

Moss, M., Hewitt, S., Moss, L., & Keith, W. (2008, January). Modulation of cognitive performance and mood by aromas of peppermint and ylang-ylang. The International journal of neuroscience. https://pubmed.ncbi.nlm.nih.gov/18041606/

Murphy, M., Eliot, K., Heuertz, R., & Weiss, E. (2012, April). Whole beetroot consumption acutely improves running performance. Journal of the Academy of Nutrition and Dietetics. https://pubmed.ncbi.nlm.nih.gov/22709704/

National Sleep Foundation. (2021, February 15). How much sleep do you really need? National Sleep Foundation. https://www.thensf.org/how-many-hours-of-sleep-do-you-really-need/

Naturopathic. (2022, May 24). 5 herbs to boost your memory - CNM college of naturopathic medicine. CNM - Diploma Courses in Nutrition, Herbal Medicine, Acupuncture, and Natural Chef. https://www.naturopathy-uk.com/news/news-cnm-blog/blog/2022/05/23/5-herbs-to-boost-your-memory/

Oliynyk, S., & Oh, S. (2013, April). Actoprotective effect of ginseng: Improving mental and physical performance. Journal of ginseng research. https://www.ncbi.nlm.nih.gov/pmc/articles/PMC3659633/

Osborn, C. O. (2019, March 8). Headache tea: Best herbal teas for a headache and where to find T. Healthline. https://www.healthline.com/health/headache-tea

Park, S., & Lee, J. (2021, December 15). Modulation of hair growth promoting effect by natural products. Pharmaceutics. https://www.ncbi.nlm.nih.gov/pmc/articles/PMC8706577/

Pervin, M., Unno, K., Ohishi, T., Tanabe, H., Miyoshi, N., & Nakamura, Y. (2018, May 29). Beneficial effects of green tea catechins on neurodegenerative diseases. Molecules (Basel, Switzerland). https://www.ncbi.nlm.nih.gov/pmc/articles/PMC6099654/

Petre, A. (2023, January 11). 7 health benefits of Yerba Mate (backed by science). Healthline. https://www.healthline.com/nutrition/8-benefits-of-yerba-mate

Petre, A. (2023, May 7). Which benefits of chasteberry are backed by science? Healthline. https://www.healthline.com/nutrition/vitex

Phoemsapthawee, J., Ammawat, W., Prasertsri, P., Sathalalai, P., & Leelayuwat, N. (2022, October 26). Does Gotu Kola supplementation improve cognitive function, inflammation, and oxidative stress more than multicomponent exercise alone? - A randomized controlled study. Journal of exercise rehabilitation. https://www.ncbi.nlm.nih.gov/pmc/articles/PMC9650315/

Pietrangelo, A. (2018, June 7). St. John's Wort: The Benefits and the dangers. Healthline. https://www.healthline.com/health-news/is-st-johns-wort-safe-080615

Pokrywka, A., Obmiński, Z., Malczewska-Lenczowska, J., Fijałek, Z., Turek-Lepa, E., & Grucza, R. (2014, July 8). Insights into supplements with Tribulus terrestris used by athletes. Journal of human kinetics. https://www.ncbi.nlm.nih.gov/pmc/articles/PMC4120469/

Poswal, F. S. (2019, September). Herbal teas and their health benefits: A scoping review - researchgate. https://www.researchgate.net/publication/334061714

Prasad, S., Aggarwal, B.B. (2011) Herbal Medicine: Biomolecular and Clinical Aspects. 2nd edition. https://www.ncbi.nlm.nih.gov/books/NBK92752/

Raman, R. (2022, June 9). 6 benefits of stinging nettle (plus side effects). Healthline. https://www.healthline.com/nutrition/stinging-nettle

Raman, R. (2023, February 16). 9 herbs and spices that fight inflammation. Healthline. https://www.healthline.com/nutrition/anti-inflammatory-herbs

Richter, A. (2023, May). 11 scientifically proven health benefits of ginger. Healthline. https://www.healthline.com/nutrition/11-proven-benefits-of-ginger

Roland, J. (2019, March 8). Which teas can be used for constipation relief?. Healthline. https://www.healthline.com/health/digestive-health/tea-for-constipation

Roschek, B., Fink, R. C., McMichael, M., & Alberte, R. S. (2009). Nettle extract (Urtica dioica) affects key receptors and enzymes associated with allergic rhinitis. Phytotherapy Research, 23(7), 920-926.

Ruggeri, C. (2023, May 31). 11 best herbal tea options. Dr. Axe. https://draxe.com/nutrition/herbal-tea-benefits/

Saenghong, N., Wattanathorn, J., Muchimapura, S., Tongun, T., Piyavhatkul, N., Banchonglikitkul, C., & Kajsongkram, T. (2012). Zingiber officinale improves cognitive function of the middle-aged healthy women. Evidence-based complementary and alternative medicine : eCAM. https://www.ncbi.nlm.nih.gov/pmc/articles/PMC3253463/

Sah, A., Naseef, P. P., Kuruniyan, M. S., Jain, G. K., Zakir, F., & Aggarwal, G. (2022, October 19). A comprehensive study of therapeutic applications of chamomile. Pharmaceuticals (Basel, Switzerland). https://www.ncbi.nlm.nih.gov/pmc/articles/PMC9611340/

Serafini, M. (n.d.). The NCBI Handbook - NCBI Bookshelf. https://www.ncbi.nlm.nih.gov/books/NBK143764/

Shah, S., Sander, S., White, M., & Rinaldi, M. (2007, July). Evaluation of echinacea for the prevention and treatment of the common cold: A meta-analysis. The Lancet. Infectious diseases. https://pubmed.ncbi.nlm.nih.gov/17597571/

Silberstein, R. B., Pipingas, A., Song, J., Camfield, D. A., Nathan, P. J., & Stough, C. (2011). Examining brain-cognition effects of ginkgo biloba extract: Brain activation in the left temporal and left prefrontal cortex in an object working memory task. Evidence-based complementary and alternative medicine : eCAM. https://www.ncbi.nlm.nih.gov/pmc/articles/PMC3166615/

Singh, B. N., Shankar, S., & Srivastava, R. K. (2011, December 15). Green tea catechin, epigallocatechin-3-gallate (EGCG): Mechanisms, perspectives and clinical applications. Biochemical pharmacology. https://www.ncbi.nlm.nih.gov/pmc/articles/PMC4082721/

Singh, N., Bhalla, M., de Jager, P., & Gilca, M. (2011, July). An overview on ashwagandha: A rasayana (rejuvenator) of ayurveda. African journal of traditional, complementary, and alternative medicines : AJTCAM. https://www.ncbi.nlm.nih.gov/pmc/articles/PMC3252722/

Sipsby. Immune-boosting teas for cold and flu season. Sips by. (n.d.). https://www.sipsby.com/blogs/seasonal-features/immune-boosting-teas-for-cold-and-flu-season#citrus

Sowbhagya, H. B. (2013). Chemistry, technology, and nutraceutical functions of fennel (Foeniculum vulgare Mill.): A review. Journal of food science and technology, 50(3), 429-438. doi: 10.1007/s13197-011-0365-1

Spencer, S., Korosi, A., Laye, S., Shukitt-Hake, B., & Barrientos, R. M. (2017, December). Food for thought: How nutrition impacts cognition and emotion. NPJ science of food. https://pubmed.ncbi.nlm.nih.gov/31304249/.

Srivastava, J. K., Shankar, E., & Gupta, S. (2010). Chamomile: A herbal medicine of the past with bright future. Molecular Medicine Reports, 3(6), 895-901.

Stieg, C. (2018, April). How Reishi Mushroom Powder Benefits Health, Brain Focus. https://www.refinery29.com/en-us/2018/04/196065/reishi-mushrooms-health-benefits

Streit, L. (2021, March 3). Meadowsweet Herb: Benefits, uses, tea, and more. Healthline. https://www.healthline.com/nutrition/meadowsweet-herb

Suni, E. (2023, March 31). What is sleep hygiene? Sleep Foundation. https://www.sleepfoundation.org/sleep-hygiene

Tamim Teas. (2021, March 17). Lion's mane, Reishi, and chaga - oh my! comparing 3 popular medicinal mushrooms. https://tamimteas.com/blogs/mushroom-tea/lion-s-mane-reishi-and-chaga-oh-my-comparing-3-popular-medicinal-mushrooms

Team, D. H. (2023, June 5). Best (and worst) ways to Sweeten Your Food. Cleveland Clinic. https://health.clevelandclinic.org/5-best-and-worst-sweeteners-your-dietitians-picks/

Team, H. (2020, April 22). Feeling dizzy? try herbal remedies for vertigo. How to Cure. https://howtocure.com/herbs-for-vertigo/

Team, T. H. E. (2020, April 13). 11 reasons to use lemongrass essential oil. Healthline. https://www.healthline.com/health/lemongrass-essential-oil

Tiralongo, E., Wee, S. S., & Lea, R. A. (2016, March 24). Elderberry supplementation reduces cold duration and symptoms in air-travellers: A randomized, double-blind placebo-controlled clinical trial. Nutrients. https://www.ncbi.nlm.nih.gov/pmc/articles/PMC4848651/

University of Maryland Medical Center. (n.d.). White willow bark. Retrieved from https://www.umm.edu/health/medical/altmed/herb/white-willow-bark

van de Walle, G. (2023, March 31). 7 proven health benefits of rhodiola rosea. Healthline. https://www.healthline.com/nutrition/rhodiola-rosea

Venables, M., Hulston, C., Cox, H., & Jeukendrup, A. (2008, March). Green tea extract ingestion, fat oxidation, and glucose tolerance in healthy humans.

The American journal of clinical nutrition. https://pubmed.ncbi.nlm.nih.gov/18326618/

Wack, M. (2022, September 15). Top 9 peppermint tea benefits: Sleep, memory, and more. ArtfulTea. https://artfultea.com/blogs/wellness/peppermint-tea-benefits

Wahab, S., Annadurai, S., Abullais, S. S., Das, G., Ahmad, W., Ahmad, M. F., Kandasamy, G., Vasudevan, R., Ali, M. S., & Amir, M. (2021, December 14). glycyrrhiza glabra (LICORICE): A comprehensive review on its phytochemistry, biological activities, clinical evidence and toxicology. Plants (Basel, Switzerland). https://www.ncbi.nlm.nih.gov/pmc/articles/PMC8703329/

White, L. B. (n.d.). 9 herbs for Healthy Eyes - mother earth living. Mother Earth Living - Healthy Life, Natural Beauty. https://www.motherearthliving.com/health-and-wellness/ask-the-herbalist-herbs-for-healthy-eyes/

Wong, C. (2023, March 22). 7 best herbs and spices for memory and Brain Health. Verywell Mind. https://www.verywellmind.com/best-herbs-and-spices-for-brain-health-4047818

Xing, D., Yoo, C., Gonzalez, D., Jenkins, V., Nottingham, K., Dickerson, B., Leonard, M., Ko, J., Faries, M., Kephart, W., Purpura, M., Jäger, R., Sowinski, R., Rasmussen, C. J., & Kreider, R. B. (2022, September 20). Effects of acute ashwagandha ingestion on cognitive function. International journal of environmental research and public health. https://www.ncbi.nlm.nih.gov/pmc/articles/PMC9565281/

Zhang, S., Takano, J., Murayama, N., Tominaga, M., Abe, T., Park, I., Seol, J., Ishihara, A., Tanaka, Y., Yajima, K., Suzuki, Y., Suzuki, C., Fukusumi, S., Yanagisawa, M., Kokubo, T., & Tokuyama, K. (2020, November 28). Subacute ingestion of caffeine and oolong tea increases fat oxidation without affecting energy expenditure and sleep architecture: A randomized, placebo-controlled, double-blinded cross-over trial. Nutrients. https://www.ncbi.nlm.nih.gov/pmc/articles/PMC7760339/

Made in the USA
Columbia, SC
23 October 2024

44969195R00122